FRED BASON'S THIRD DIARY

FRED
BASON by

NICOLAS
BENTLEY

FRED BASON'S

3rd

DIARY

Edited and with an Introduction by
MICHAEL SADLEIR

ANDRE DEUTSCH

FIRST PUBLISHED 1955 BY
ANDRE DEUTSCH LIMITED
12-14 CARLISLE STREET SOHO SQUARE
LONDON W1
ALL RIGHTS RESERVED
PRINTED IN GREAT BRITAIN BY
TONBRIDGE PRINTERS LIMITED
TONBRIDGE KENT

To 5207 who asked for 'Another Basonfull'
My Thanks for your Encouragement
And to Brand New Readers
May this suit your Taste

'Humour is the salt of life'

INTRODUCTION

FRED BASON is now forty-seven years of age (he was born in 1907) and this is the third volume to be published of extracts from a diary which, off and on, he has kept since his early teens. The opening entry in the first published volume (that edited by Nicolas Bentley in 1950) is dated 1921, and records the kindly generosity of Marie Lloyd to a diminutive shaver who laid in wait for her at the Camberwell Palace and asked for her autograph. The second extract contained in *Diary I* and the first contained in *Diary II* (edited by L. A. G. Strong in 1952) are dated 1922. Of these extracts the first is an engaging medley of remarks about second-hand bookselling, a new suit, Kid Lewis and G. K. Chesterton, the second is about boxing and boxers. And now, as a Prologue to *Diary III* are offered two further fragments from 1922, a lament for Marie Lloyd just dead, and a tentative excursion into literature under the guidance of Sir Edmund Gosse.

To read these primitive paragraphs virtually written by an almost-child with no education to speak of, a child put out to work when just turned fourteen, is to feel at the very outset of one's acquaintance with Fred Bason admiration and affection. This little creature has guts and to spare; he has also, though he may not thank me for saying so, an underlying pathos which, even as he climbs the ladder of success, never fails to command our respect.

'As he climbs the ladder of success...' Too grandiloquent a phrase? I think not. It has been a steep climb and a long one to the popularity and widespread reputation of today, from the furniture factory in which an undergrown cockney shrimp struggled with physical labour grossly beyond his strength, and, at the age of fifteen, wrote despairingly in his diary: 'I cannot stick this work. I want to be a writer and a seller of books'.

He added: 'I know I can make a go when I have a bit of money'. The three volumes of his *Diary* tell the story of how Fred has made a 'go'; and though some passages may be thought wearisome, some even distasteful, the story is a record of achievement which may fairly be termed unique.

What progress has Fred made between *Diary I* and *Diary III*? Has his style altered for better or for worse? From the beginning his writing was shrewd, energetic and perpetually lively. He has the appealing pertness of a cocksparrow, flipping about London at all hours, pecking in the gutters, ruffling on the roof-trees – at once cheeky and forlorn, at once gregarious and desperately lonely. Especially 'lonely', for Fred has never had anyone to help him. What he has made of himself is of his own making.

And what *has* he made? Readers of this third *Diary* will be conscious of a more ambitious, more 'literary' handling of material, so that the *Diary* tends to become a conscious self-valuation in diary form rather than a day-by-day chronicle of a young mind's awakening and eager awareness of things which happen. There is a greater proportion of what may be termed 'set pieces' – extracts from radio talks, contributed articles, lectures to clubs – and a corresponding reduction of entries inspired by mere curiosity and a volatile delight in exclamatory impertinence. They will further note the gradual elimination of second-hand bookselling as a major preoccupation, although autograph collecting maintains its interest, and they will observe an elaboration of anecdotes and pen-portraiture.

These signs of a diarist-coming-of-age are welcome as evidence of Fred's progress towards complete self-confidence. But they are not all of them to the advantage of the journal as a whole. Here and there the stress laid on the ego is too heavy; for which reason we are doubly grateful for his mischievous readiness to exploit, to his own amusing disadvantage, a few adventures on the fringes of venery.

★　★　★

The incidental narratives which adorn the following pages vary in value, and are the more interesting for doing so. The first prize I award without hesitation to 'Southwark Serenade' which, the more strongly to emphasise its quality, I have placed at the end of the book. It is not a diary entry in the ordinary sense; but it is a compendium of Fred's talents as a diarist – his eye for incident and effect; his ear for noise and chatter; his stubborn attachment to Walworth, his home-town, despite a keen awareness of its drawbacks as a residential area; his lively capacity for seeing himself as a nimble and semi-comic midget slipping in and out of the vast labyrinth of London.

As Prologue is presented another set-piece – a pen-portrait of Lizzie, Fred's gallant landlady, housekeeper and ministering angel. This affectionate tribute claims no such universal significance as 'Southwark Serenade'; but it has the warmth of love and gratitude, and can suitably preface the passages from the *Diary* in which Lizzie makes appearance and which show her to be unmistakably a major character in Fred's crowded chronicle of friends and acquaintances.

Of other personalities and episodes forming part of the *Diary* proper your attention is especially invited to the encounter on the Thames embankment with Sir Frank Dicksee, P.R.A.; the tea-party with Mrs Belloc Lowndes and her cats; the pleasant reminiscence of John Drinkwater; the bet with Edgar Wallace; a lunch with Stanley Rubinstein at Kettner's, which compares nicely with that of a year earlier at Verrey's (*Diary II*, page 121) and is enjoyed as unashamedly as any host could desire; the long and vivid account of an evening at the Café de Paris by generous invitation of Noel Coward; and, to wind up, the sensational day at the point-to-point with Colonel Lyon.

Being personally involved in Fred's entry for a day early in 1953, I ask permission briefly to intervene as a diary character rather than as an editor. The point at issue between us is fairly stated by Fred; and he tries, although reluctantly, to meet my request for some reference to W. Pett Ridge, whom I knew well and regard as a cockney novelist of real importance, the best of whose work should return to favour with the next swing of the pendulum of taste. Further, as a writer about London, Pett Ridge was absolutely up Fred's street. Walworth, Hoxton, Bethnal Green, Paddington, Highgate, Kentish Town –

he knew and loved them all, relishing their humour, their impudence, their naïve emotionalism. But Fred deplores cluttering up his *Diary* with 'very dead authors of very dead books' and includes Pett Ridge in this lugubrious regiment. Yet George Arliss, Mrs Langtry, Martin Harvey, James Agate, Miss Braddon and others find a place in the *Diary* although they are no longer alive, and the continued vitality of their artistic achievement is anybody's guess. So I doubt our disagreement being very profound after all. As for Pett Ridge, Fred with characteristic shrewdness says he looked like a horse-dealer (as indeed he did), but it was Fred's bad luck never to hear him say 'a single funny thing'. Pett Ridge's speciality was the collecting and rendering of cockney conversations – fragments overheard on buses or on crowded pavements, long narratives of misfortune confided to him in chance encounters – related with perfect gravity, reproduced verbatim and in faultless vernacular. Fred has a few such 'over-hearings' in his *Diary* and they are well enough in their way; but of inexhaustible material in the grand manner Pett Ridge was the master purveyor, and as such should be remembered.

★ ★ ★

It would do this *Diary* and its author an injustice to end my Preface without a brief dissertation on the unregenerate topic of Fred and the ladies. This topic, as treated by him, provides an agreeable counter-irritant – humorous, pathetic, cruel, even macabre – to undue prolongation of trivial chat about 'famous' nonentities. A large proportion of Fred's fan mail comes from women. Many clamour to make his acquaintance; and, being an obliging optimist, he accepts invitations to tea or supper or meets them by appointment. Sometimes they feed him a nice meal with interesting conversation which he enjoys. Sometimes they come carrying a parcel, fully prepared for dalliance, and frighten him to death by their over-urgency. Sometimes, at a street corner, they offer a tête-à-tête on a business footing, only to find they have to deal with a tough and experienced little cockney who knows most of the answers. The disillusionments and narrow escapes and horrid contrasts between photographs supplied and nature's handiwork constitute a sequence of adventures-in-prospect, of generosity ill-requited, of vain expectations, and only very occasionally of happy consummation or unblemished *camaraderie*.

Fred bears his disappointments with stoicism, although he can be badly hurt by cold ingratitude. At the other end of the scale, when he thinks himself tricked, the woman responsible becomes swiftly and painfully aware of what L. A. G. Strong has charitably termed 'the touch of hardness' underlying Fred's 'quick sympathies and warm heart'.

MICHAEL SADLEIR

PROLOGUE: LIZZIE

A MAN is not much good on his own and I have been a very fortunate man for the past twenty years because I have had an admirable landlady, Lizzie. I am frequently called the cockney Boswell and if it weren't for Lizzie, who is my Johnson, there would never have been any diary – or any me, because on many occasions she has saved my life by nursing me through serious illnesses and I owe her more than anything could repay. Her real name is Mrs Elizabeth Keep. Like me she is a cockney, and again like me she is very small...smaller even than my own five foot five. She is seven stone of courage and common sense. Nothing in the war got her down and she was in London all through the blitz.

But I've got no wish to talk about war. I want to tell you about Liz, to paint a sort of pen picture. As a preface for my remarks, and for her protection, I must tell you that she did not go to school and her only schooling came from her daughter in later years and from the hard school of life.

Liz is, like all cockneys, seldom at a loss for an answer. When I said long ago that I had been talking to Lord Reading she immediately said, 'I hope you brought home some biscuits!' She looks upon the Luton girls' choir as the best advert for British *hats* in the world. She don't like their singing for she says that too many are singing the *same* words at the *same* time – that you cannot sort the words from the noise!

When we went to a high-class 'do', she saw a woman in an off-the-shoulder gown and the woman said, 'Do you like it?' she said 'Like what, ma'am? Seems to me that you are getting ready to have a good *wash!*'

We get a great many world famous folks call upon us – for we both have a scrap of fame. When last year Ruth Draper called and had tea with us Liz said, 'You can *see* that she is a REAL lady – she's keeping her hat on for tea!' And when Nicolas Bentley called in a nice looking car she told me to print with ink on a piece of paper 'C.I.D.' and stick it on the back of the car so that the wise boys of the village left it alone. When a jeweller pal gave her some pearls this Christmas she said, 'I was thinking of asking the other Elizabeth if she could spare a few things from the Crown Jewels . . . but she can keep 'em now to sell to American visitors'. We had an American visitor who called my Lizzie a piece of Dresden china, meaning that she looked dainty and fragile – and Liz ups and says, 'Dresden is *German* – British china or nothing, IF you PLEASE!'

Lizzie has many favourites. Gracie Fields is one of them because she sings like she is *at* your fireside. She likes Max Wall, the comedian, because he does not have to make *im*proper jokes to get seemly merriment. She adores the actor Alec Clunes 'because you can nearly be asleep and still hear every word he says . . . and because he's handsome and *still* a man!'

I am very fortunate to have such a kind landlady. She is a great use to my EGO – everything I write is to her a

Masterpiece and she just don't know how I does it. But once I was writing about the weather and using the word which Shaw used so effectively I wrote that it was a bloody cold day – and she said, 'Just cause Shaw used this unseemly word is no reason for you – he had a beard as well – but if you had a beard I would cut it off'. I asked why not a beard and she replied, 'They are only to hide scraggy necks, and for dirty old men who don't like neck washing!' I told this to Shaw and how he laughed – and then said, 'She has a great deal of wisdom!' And that is what she has. You so seldom get the obvious reply. I have known her to say when it's raining very hard that the angels are crying as someone is doing wrong. This is a nice phrase. And upon a sunny day she will say that the fairies are dancing.

She does believe in fairies. Lizzie is very superstitious. She would not go underneath a ladder for any sum; she reads her fortune and mine in the teacups very often. If the thing foretold in the cups doesn't come true right away she blames it on the civil servants who have been messing about with fate.

She is very brave and loyal. She is also very gentle. Many times during the past twenty years I have been desperately ill and but for her tender nursing I would have kicked the bucket.

I don't think that I've ever seen her read a book entirely through, with the exception of my own writings. She reads the first ten pages – and then the last five, and if they don't sort of link up, then it is no good, too much description and not enough action. Her favourite author is me, and next to me it's Somerset Maugham – because as she says the man gets on with the tale with no messing about and you know where you are. Yet her two favourite novels are *Fanny by Gaslight* (Sadleir) and *Heaven and Herbert Common* (Tilsley).

Of course, Lizzie is very proud of being a Londoner, and although she likes a week at the seaside once a year she likes to come back to her Walworth and her neighbours. When I am very busy she often takes my overseas fans and friends around the town as a friendly guide. Her part of London is rather the London of Charles Dickens and she knows many of the literary associations of Dickens' time.

I have yet to find a soul who does not like my landlady. She is a TREASURE–and I wouldn't swop her for the most glamorous piece of young female skirt of today. I want to marry. But where is there an equal to Lizzie?

¶ *1922. Fred is fifteen*

I am wearing a black arm band around me arm this day because Marie Lloyd died two days ago. I would have worn said same band yesterday but I had to buy it (6d from a shop in Waterloo Road) and I could not get there yesterday and I did not wish to ask my mother to make me one.

With the passing away of Marie Lloyd a bit of real old London has gone forever and won't come again. She ain't got no equal, not as far as I sees. Six times I saw and heard her and four of them times I waited after the show to see her come out of stage door. Very stylish lady and a real matey smile for one and all. With my own eyes I saw her give money to man who looked as if he knew real how to drink, or perhaps he was ill? It was a lot of money. They said that she was easy to touch, which means that she gave without carefull investigation, not like charities in Southwark what want to know all your ins and outs and reckon also about the mole on your shoulder before they gives a penny. Not that my mother or father would ever accept a penny piece from charity. But perhaps giving made Marie Lloyd happy.

There are some people who gets pleasure from giving

gifts. I have not given anything myself yet but sweets to girls – because I never seem to have much after my mother has taken from me wage packet for this and that. Her name was Tillie Wood (Marie, not my mother who was Annie Blount before she met my poor dad) and they says that Tillie Wood and very often *did!* Thats supposed to be a joke. My mother said at tea last night that Marie was vulgar but my mother says a lot of things and some of them are very cruel like me being a trouble since the day I was born to her and she wished that I was dead. She wishes me dead nearly once a week. I am unwanted by her. Marie had two sisters Alice and Rosie. I like Alice lots best after Marie. Last time I talked to George at the Holborn Empire he told me that Marie got six hundred pounds for just one week appearing at Cardiff. George also said that she got an average wage of two fifty a week and had had that average for many years so she could afford to be generous. She had it. Some have and don't ever give. She gave me a photo of her and Alec Hurley. She'd been sent it she said and it was signed by both of them. I will always keep this as a souvenir of a Grand Lady. I shall keep my black band on for one week and not tell who it's for as I don't like being laughed at. You can be real sorry for some one dying who ain't a real relation. I don't see why you have to be sorry just when relations die. You cant pick relations and some of mine stink awfull.

¶ *Still 1922, two weeks later*

They say that forty-eight thousand people was at Marie Lloyd's funeral. Who counted them? I wasn't there as I was at awfull work in a carpentry factory at Camberwell. It's a bad job. Slave work and I am feeling real sick of it. I have to pull the planks out from the planing machine and I am covered with chips all day and the noise is awfull. My mother keeps saying that I am lazy. She is very hard. She has no love at all for me. The noise of the job rings all the night and I breath saw dust. I get 21s a week. I work from 8 till 7.30 with an hour for dinner and a five minute tea break at four. My mother takes 18s for food, 1s for my clothes etc. My 2s soon goes. A few books and once at flicks and all gone.

I want to get the autograph of Kate Carney before she dies. She is hale like right now. You cannot get dead people. I have written to film star Norman Kerry for a signed photo. He's a handsome film man but not a cowboy. I must put this down. Mr Harvey, my schoolmaster of a year ago, said once, When you crib a little bit of a man's writing its Cheating but when you crib lots of his work it is called *Research* – This is called a epigram. I would like to crib some Arnold Bennett and J. Conrad to practice. I cannot stick this work, I want to be a writer and a seller of books. I know I can make a go when I have a bit of money. I must get money. I just got to get out of this work.

¶ *June 1922*

I have this day read a book by Edmund Gosse called *Aspects and Impressions* published by Cassell at 7s 6d.

It was given to me as a free gift by a nasty old man. I write nasty because this bloke took snuff in a most untidy manner and also because he carried in his wallet pictures of boys with no clothes on. I would sooner have a Venus photo. He gave me the book because it was given to him. I accepted his book but said that I have no wish to meet him ever again because he gives me the shudders. He has been asking me to get him certain titles of books which I am sure are nasty books and I do not ever intend to deal in indecent books.

This book *Aspects and Impressions* is about people like H. James, G. Eliot (funny old dame) and Samuel Butler who would be a great author in any age. I have heard of these people and some I've read. But it's also about Ram Bouillitt and Francois Malherbe who are very new to me. The book is good class and Gosse man knows what he is writing about. He is a C.B. but I don't know what C.B. stands for. (Might be Clever Bloke for he is certainly that and I am very sure that I shall never write impressions in the same class.) I would much have liked to have been invited to tea by the funny old woman with the man's name George Eliot. I am sure that she would have told me such a lot that I don't know. Yet I get the impression from Gosse's impression that she would not have been very nice to know.

I must also record that pretty well every page of this book was snuff-dirty finger marks what a rubber would not get out. It gave me a shudder to try to read it. I think I would enjoy this book better at seventy-one. It will go into my booksack tomorrow and I will accept any sum that I am offered on my travels. If I can get two shillings I shall be gratefull as I see that I can get a Maugham for that money (which sells better). Guy Boothby seems to

be wanted – if the Maugham is gone after I get the cash
I'll buy Boothby. I have the toothache this day but dread
the awfull wait at dentists. Life is very good ... that's my
impressions. I have no aspects. I must look that one up.
What is aspects?

¶ *November 1923. Fred is 16*

Yesterday I treated myself to a gallery seat at St James
theatre and witnessed George Arliss in *The Green
Goddess*. This is a four act play what takes place in a
region beyond the Himalayas and for me it can keep itself
there. I am bound to say that G. Arliss is what is called a
powerfull actor and he holds attention but I liked Isobel
Elsom, who was very pretty.

G. Arliss is called The Raja of Rukh in the play. I could
have called him something – he would not give me his
signature – just ignored me – passed like as if I was dust.
Acting a raja in St James St won't get him anywhere. He
has a weirdish face and a very fierce looking nose. Isobel
got nice nose and signed my book. Play was written by
William Archer. I am told he is dead so I can't get him
to sign. The music between Act 3 and 4 was Four Indian
Love Lyrics and lovely and sweet.

¶ *June 4th 1924*

The Derby has just been won by a Derby which is right
and proper – What they call Poetic justice. Lord Derby's
horse Sansovino won the race by six clear lengths from
St Germans (owned by Lord Astor). This is the first time

a Derby has won the Derby in the 137 years that it was founded by his family.

It rained all the whole day there, I am told, and it rained all the day here in Walworth. I did not back the winner – but my father did and he's putting money in the post office for me when he gets paid tomorrow as he says it's better to give to me than give it back to the Bookies. My father is very clever at horse racing and knows all about handicaps but on the whole is so clever that he works slaving hard to earn about £3 a week repairing the harness of horses and loses at least a third of it on horses in an afternoon.

One day I will give serious attention to betting and I will win all my dad has lost and when I have won it I will buy a whole house and no Bookie will ever take that away because I shall never again bet more than 10s in any one year. With self control I am sure a bloke can bet to win if he is not greedy. It's only by greed that betters lose their bets. Getting rich quick is quick way to Folly or something.

¶ *September 1925. Fred is 18*

I have just seen a lady who was once known as The Jersey Lily. Her name is Langtry. She looked a very washed out Lily. A case of a lady outliving her fame and beauty (some old ladies are very handsome). I put forward my large autograph album at His Majesties Theatre and was extremely polite in my request for her signature but she said NO, You are late, and sailed off with a silly bit of ribbon in her hair. I can't see how on earth I was late, when this was the very first time I was told it was Lily Langtry and seen her in person. She had a lot of air but so few graces when she refused my polite request. When a copper, who was helping with the crowd, asked me who she was and I said that she was the Jersey Lily he laughed and said she seemed a *bit off*. How right he was. People who were once someone and who have outlived their famous days ought to grow old gracefully and BE VERY PLEASED WHEN THEY ARE REMEMBERED by folks young enough to be their sons.

¶ *September 1925. Fred is 18*

Not been much doing of late, diary, but before I forget it must just put down that Sir John Martin Harvey obliged this week with his autograph. He looks more like an actor than any other actor I've ever seen but his wife looks less like an actress than any other woman. I would have taken her for a dealer in old clothes or maybe a midwife. Any rate there she was with him, and as she seemed to be wanting to be asked as well, bless her old heart, I asked her as well. She scrawled an impressive looking signature which looked like N— something de Silver. I looked at it and then at her. Is there anything wrong with it she asked? No mam, said me, if that happens to be your name. She assured me that it was her name and asked what on earth I had thought it was. I replied that (since she'd asked me and beg pardon for any rudeness what was not intended by me) it seemed as if she had written 'I've got no SILVER' in Italian. They both laughed at that and showed lots of false teeth. I was just going off when Sir John called me back and he said 'My boy. A laugh is valuable. My wife may have no silver – but I have', and he handed me a two shillings piece. That was proper nice of him. I spent it seeing their show (which I hadn't seen. I'd only got their autographs because they happened to be very famous stage people and not because I had ever seen or admired their work). I only know that Martin Harvey did something called *The Only Way*, which seems to be the only thing he really knows how to do. But they were very nice homely people. At first Sir John seems almost unapproachable and unbending but thats only HIS way. Cor – I seem to have made a pun.

¶ *January 14 1926*

A cyclist in Poplar dropped his wallet. Four boys saw the wallet dropped. They called out but the cyclist didn't hear so they took it to the post office. It contained forty pounds in notes. They were just leaving when in came the cyclist seeking his wallet. He was able to convince the post office people it was his. He gave the four boys one halfpenny each! Honesty is the *best* policy … outside Poplar?

¶ *July 10 1926*

From the Hotel Metropole show called *The Midnight Follies* I have been sent this day a signed photo of Cortez and Peggy. They are billed as 'Admittedly the worlds most wonderful dancers'. This is the very first time I've ever seen the word 'Admittedly' before the worlds greatest

and so it must go into my diary. But who admits it? I have
been friendly for some weeks now with the Peggy side
of the team. Her name is Milly Peggy. She is the first lady
I've come upon who has a girl's name either way round
and could use her name either way – being Peggy Milly
or Milly Peggy. Personally, I'd take her anyway, but Mr
Cortez got there first and so really she is Mrs Cortez and
likes people to think that she is Spanish.

I had the opportunity to go to the Hotel, but I explained
that my clothes would not fit and my speech would give
me away, and that in any case I knew me place, which
was OUTSIDE watching the Toffs, NOT inside trying to
ape them. I had to supply *Old Wives Tales* to Mrs Cortez,
which shows that she's not only a dancer of note but got
BRAINS as well.

¶ *1926 as it was to me – the year as a year*

I always find pleasure at the close of any year to refer
back to my diaries and pick out some of the highlights
of it. That way I re-live many of them.

Started the year by going to The Coliseum to variety.
The turns were Tom Clare at a piano, Robert Chisolm, a
very manly singer, Sissle and Blake, two coloured gentle-
men who sing and play piano, and a jazz band called Bert
Ralton's Havana Band, although how many, if any of them,
have ever seen Havana I had and still have me doubts. Tom
Clare was the best act. I was able to get the autographs
of The Trix Sisters this night, also Margaret Yarde and
Bert Coote, a very funny looking cove. All in all a nice
opening to New Year for I saw a film called *The Unholy*

Three (Lon Chaney, Victor McLagen and May Busch) in the afternoon.

The one sensation of January was the comeback of Ernie Rice the lightweight boxer. They say they never come back but Rice knocked the stuffing out of Billy Bird in two rounds and is now to fight Harry Mason for the championship he lost. Ernie Rice and me are friendly, Harry Mason and me are friendly – who do I cheer for? Or do I go and say, GO ON BOTH OF YOU?

February 9th. I met Sir Harry Lauder for the first time in person. I found him to be a very amiable celebrity but I could not understand much of his lingo cause he talked Scotch. He was with Harry Tate. I was lucky and got both of them to sign and Sir H. L. asked me why I do this, and I said that some chaps collect sweethearts and some chaps signatures. I'm the last lot and its cheaper than fur coats. Ah, maybe, maybe he said. Then I thought that he'd say a mouthfull that I could record – but what did he say? He said 'Ah Maybe, Maybe' *twice more*. He was dressed up Scotch and he had a kilt on. Harry Tate had a thick fine overcoat on. Me had my overcoat on for it was a very chilly night but Harry Lauder didn't have an overcoat, just a brown tweed jacket and kilt and yet it was us who seemed perished with the cold and Sir Harry the one who looked warm and rosy and merry and bright. I wonder how he does it. Maybe he's Scotch outside and very much more Scotch inside in large drops.

February also saw Harry Mason beat Ernie Rice after a good fight and the great Teddy Baldock lick Frankie Ash. Only other thing of interest was in this month I met Bransby Williams. Said that he knew Walworth very well.

I saw Alice Deylisa in a funny sketch in March. She is kissing a man. Suddenly she worries and says, I wonder if George will come in. Oh no, he's in Leeds, it's alright. But George does come in as they are kissing. There is a great big row, a regular scene. George says he will leave her forever. Alice says that she was so lonely, she begs forgiveness. The first man leaves and George is supposed to make love to Alice. He does so, at first reluctantly and then with more ardour, for who can resist Alice Deylisa? ... and then there comes another knock at the door and Alice says, MY HUSBAND ... Black out. And I bet that everyone in that theatre thought that George was her husband till she said these two words.

In this merry month I also saw R. Valentino in *The Eagle*. I can realise why the women fall for this ex-convict dish washer. He really is uncommonly handsome.

On Thursday March 25th my grand dad Granpa Bason died after many weeks of painfull illness. A very good and kind man. Perhaps too good. There was a prayer meeting every time he called on us. We all had to get down on our knees whilst he did a lot of praying for our souls and it made me trousers so baggy.

April was nice for the meeting with Clarice Mayne at The Coliseum. Big strapping woman and lots of charm. I did a big deal in the novels of E. V. Savi this month. They are good sellers and I gambled three quarters of all my cash on a big load of them. I do not fear the result. Not quite so sure as E. M. Dell would be but Savi is reliable.

I had a nice racehorse win this month when Kyra won the Great Met at ten to one. Somehow I had a feeling that Kyra was Indian like the romances of E. V. Savi and would be a title for one of her books and having gambled on the books, why not a horse. I won ten pounds but if I'd lost I'd have had 1s 7d in the world.

Monday May 3rd saw the Greatest of all strikes. Special constables. Troops leave stopped. Trouble everywhere. But it proves the Power of the WORKER. It ended on the 14th but no worker should ever or will ever forget it. Nothing else equalled the strike, so nothing else will be mentioned!

¶ *1927*

I have an old man as a buyer of books off me who really does buy outlandish titles. He bought *Cosmotherapy* by a Professor E. Szekely. I asked him why and he said just curiosity. Said it was strange to him and he intended to find out all about it. Said he wanted to gain all the knowledge he could whilst in this here world to fit himself for a responsible position in the next. Oh yes those are his words. What sort of responsible position and whether it was union wages, he had no idea and I did not chip him — he was so sincere. He firmly thinks you have to pass an examination at the close of this life on all manner of subjects and pass 75% before you get to the upper school of thought in a distant world — somewhere far from ours.

¶ *January 2nd 1928. During this year Fred comes of age*

It seems to me that a big depression has set in around my part of London. The weather is indeed terrible. No one seems to be out. Not that I can blame them but no one passes or enters my little bookshop. In the last four days I have taken exactly two shillings and fourpence. Its starvation wages. I cannot even offord a bit of coal for the fire and I am burning books that come my way in lots and I found to be defective, but really they don't keep me very warm and the little fire is dead in a few minutes again.

I long to go to the Alhambra and see the magician De Biere. He is always worth seeing for he is so very serious over his act. He is also very clever and one of the few magicians whose work really does mystify me. But I havn't got the price of a gallery seat. I notice that at the Coliseum they got Noni the very funny clown and Max Wall who never fails to make me laugh. Will Hay is also in the bill but somehow having seen him three times I feel I know what he and his company will do. Still its a very good bill and as though the above ain't enough there is Gwen Farrer with her cello and Florence Smithson. Its said that Miss Farrar's old man is or was a millionaire. She's the only millionaire's daughter I have yet seen (indeed I've actually spoken to her) and I must say that she has what is known as a presence. You sort of know she is a SOMEONE. Indeed she ain't like quite anyone else on the stage or off it; which is a proper blessing for her. I'd like to be not a bit like anyone else, just be myself. But when you seem natural they think you is swanking.

I notice in the papers that Miss Gleize failed to swim the Straits of Gib yesterday. Well what on earth made her want to try . . . in this weather and all, she seems such a nice little body (I have her autograph). Lois Fuller the noted dancer died yesterday . . . most inconsiderate of her

B

seeing as how I did not have her autograph. True she was at the height of her fame long before my schooldays were over, but she might have waited I am sure I'd have got around to her in good time.

I was invited to the New Year Party of The Masons. Met a nice girl in their company. But said nothing for I have just 35 and 4 in the whole wide world, which ain't much with *mink* the price it is.

Notice that Edythe Baker the pianist is to marry in two days time. They say that she has no trouble in earning two hundred pounds a week. Now *she* would be proper lovely to marry. Looks, lots of cash and could play the piano to me when we was not doing other things. I wish her happiness. I am blooming well sure that I do not have to wish her husband-to-be *anything* – he has got the *lot*. Still I must confess that in my own heart I do not like this great inequality in the state of people. Riches in Buckingham Palace, Rags in Islington and Walworth . . .

Postman has just been. Nice photograph for me from Roy Royston – so kind of him. Wonder if he took more than 2s 4d in the past four days. I have not been lazy this day. Been repairing books and reading *Impulse* by Isobel Ostrander. Please God, just a little trade. PLEASE.

¶ *January 1928*

Last night (it's now early in the morning and I have the morning-after feeling) I went to see *The Lady of the Lamp* by R. Berkeley at the Garrick Theatre. The principles in the cast were Edith Evans and Eille Norwood (who looks far more like Sherlock Holmes than S. Holmes

would look if he was real). There was also Gwen 'F' Davies
and Leslie Banks in the play, so all the acting was good.
It's a very moving play and a page out of history.

The woman I took with me (L. Banks gave me the
tickets for nothing) cried most of the time and made her
own and then my hanky real wet – then had the blooming
sauce to say that she hadn't enjoyed herself so much for
years . . . and then in a burst of sheer kindness of heart
(for she was *not* that sort of woman) she said that I could
spend an hour in bed with her in her little flat. This I
jolly well did. We did not have a lamp and there were
no more tears. We had a really enjoyable hour. I am fast
learning that women are so strange. First you makes 'em
cry – then you can get what does you good. This somehow lines up with what a Camberwell Casanova said a
while ago – to keep your old woman you gives her a
bashing once a month, just to show her who is the boss –
then you takes her out and gets her tight. Never do it
the other way around else you loses 'em. Bashing first and
beer last and you've got 'em.

★ ★ ★

¶ *March 3rd 1929*

This night at the Strand Theatre I saw a great play
called *Rope* by Patrick Hamilton. It's a thriller and everybody cheered it. Will soon sell and be seen by the public
and how they will like it. I got the author's autograph and
by the way he signed I could guess no one had ever before
asked him for his signature. Nice sort of bloke . . . quiet
and almost shy. But knows his onions.

This show was lucky for me as I got the autographs

of Matheson Lang, Isabel Jeans, Eliot Makeham and Leslie Banks, which was a good haul.

It's bitterly cold weather. I don't often put the weather, but it's what even brass monkeys would suffer from. Yesterday was also lucky because P. G. Wodehouse sent me a signed book *Jill the Reckless* instead of just his autograph. Seems reckless with his money, but how kind.

¶ *June 1927*

This week I attended a grey-hound racing meeting at the White City. The grey-hounds run after a dummy rabbit. I believe this first racing of its sort ever in London but its been done up North. I can see this as the working man's sport and one at which I can easily make money. There are six dogs in a race and it is obvious that the one who is in Trap number One is nearest to the railings and so he has *not* so far to run as the dog on the outside trap. I judge No. 1 has a two lengths advantage over No. 6 dog and about half a length on the other four dogs – so if Number One gets clear out the trap, keeps sight of the rabbit, stays at the rails, he will win eight times out of ten.

Favourites at Grey-hounds are real Favourites and no one needs know anything about Grey-hounds – Just bet steady on Favourites and you *must* win! Or must lose. Anyrate I like the Grey-hounds and I shall go again and again.

There was quite 18,000 people at this White City first meeting and lots of celebrities there. I got several autographs but better still I won 32s above my outlay of getting there and back. The day will come when Grey-hounds will replace horses for working people – Horses, the sport of Kings, but I no like kings at any time so its Dogs for me. Point to note on parade. The Dancing Dog, the prancing Dog, The excited dog is often The Hungry Dog. This dog runs faster – he is after The Rabbit!

* * *

¶ *January 1st 1928*

This year I shall be 21. My new year resolution is to wear a buttonhole each day. I am blooming sure that I am going to be laughed at by the neighbours but I don't care. Far, far better men than I shall ever become have been laughed at and scorned – yet they make the grade. I think our drab streets need a bit of colour. I can't remember seeing in years a man of Walworth with a flower in his lapel. All they wear are union badges. I have no union. I'll wear a flower and to hell with the neighbours!

* * *

¶ *January 11th 1928*

I am beaten. This day I was asked 2s 6d for a very beautiful rose. It really was a gem – but I had to do a swift calculation and found out that if I purchased that rose I would have no money to go to the theatre this week and there is a Maugham play I really must see. Bang has gone my new year resolution!

I only got laughed at once in the ten days I've worn a flower and then by a woman who should have known better than to call me 'sissy' for she of all women *knows* I am not that! No man made a remark. Indeed, I've a sort of feeling they'd wear one as well if they had the guts to overcome their wives' sarcastic remarks.

I wonder who said it first: – 'There is a great difference between a good book and a good woman. You can always shut up a good book!' I told this joke to W. W. Jacobs on the day he gave me a copy of *The Skipper's Wooing*. It did make him laugh – and although he writes real funny books he ain't a bloke given much to laughter. I do not think I'll make a resolution next year – wait until half-crowns are more in me pocket.

¶ *March the 14th 1929*

Today I lined up in a queue at the gallery entrance of the New Theatre the whole of the day from nine in the morn till we went in at 8.15. I got the second row gallery and witnessed *The Circle of Chalk* in which the stars were Anna May Wong, film actress and George Curzon. I did not enjoy this play at all. It was far too fancifull but the production itself was fastinating and Anna looked a dream. (She has promised me a photograph). She tried to sing in this play and just cannot sing. Some one *must* tell her.

I've had this day such a nice kind letter from John Oxenham the writer. I had told him of the woman who adored his books and scrubbed floors to get the money to buy all of them. Yet you would never guess that verse appealed to her. Mary Newcombe the actress also sent a charming letter. What a lesson some could learn in good manners from both of these people. Greater they are the nicer they are. I've found that out from my hobby and I ain't found it at fault. The trade in my little bookshop is so good that I spent the whole of yesterday away from it and I am very sure that I lost nothing. What did I do? I went to the greyhounds and won money. I do tipping and forecasting winners as a sideline now. Today, for a change, I followed my own selections.

¶ *July 1st 1929*

I am very happy this here day because I've had nice letters with autographs from Aldous Huxley and Alec Coppard. Neither man would I see in person without a lot of luck, so sending stamped addressed envelope I asked. Now they have obliged me. I purchased today *The Miracle Boy* by L. Golding. *The English Miss* by R. H. Mottram, *The Caliban* by Thornton Wilder, *Saints in Sussex* by S. Kaye Smith at 3s 6d each in fine clean state. Think I can make a small but honest profit on these (after reading). Think *Miracle Boy* will be along my alley. It's about a boxer in Bermondsey. If I like it I will tell the author. I wonder if he will care? I was lucky to see St John Ervine in Haymarket; and although he seemed astonished at being asked and said that I was clever to recognise him, he signed my album.

I have to go to tea with Mrs Belloc Lowndes tomorrow. I rather dread it as might break her cup: not much of a hand at tea parties. It does seem an art to hold cup and saucer in one hand and lump of cake, and balance a plate and still carry on polite conversation. I can't sort of do it. But Mrs Lowndes is a good customer of mine with her Victorian wants. Anything Queen Vic and its a sure sale to her.

¶ *Likely 1929.   A recollection of a great artist*

It's beyond my power to date this recollection although I know it to be in the late twenties. Its put down as some sort of proof that its unwise to judge people by their clothes in London or elsewhere for that matter.

It was very late at night and I had been getting autographs at the Playhouse Theatre on the Embankment. I was feeling very satisfied with my autographic captures and at peace with the world as I walked along beside the river. Now, I am unmarried and so going home to bed only means going home to sleep and I can sleep anytime so I am in no hurry and when I come to a seat I sit me down and gaze at the river traffic.

Now there was an old man on this seat. He was a small man about my own 5′5 and of slim build like me. I could have worn his suit with ease but not with relish for he looked very untidy and indeed seedy. The only thing neat about him was a whitish Vandyck beard. He looked as if he'd seen much better days and even allowing for the time of night he looked as if a good wash would do him the world of good. He stared at me a moment and then asked if I woud spare him twopence for a cup of tea. I spared him twopence gladly for I know what a cup of tea does to help when one is blue and down.

I was just going to get up and go on my way when he asked me to spare a moment. I thought that he was going to make another touch. Well, I was flush and a bob was neither here nor there. I sat down again although it was well on midnight. He said, Why did you give me tuppence? Well mate, I replied, You asked for it and you don't look the sort of bloke who makes a habit of touching people for cash and I am pretty sure that you'd not have lowered your pride to ask unless you *really* needed it. And besides all that you have a nice white beard. He laughed. Then he said, I've been sitting here for over half an hour as an experiment. In that time I've asked seven people – passers-by, for twopence for tea and you are the first to oblige me. I do not need your money. I am an R.A. A P.R.A. in fact. Do you know what these letters stand for? I nodded. Well, my boy, my name is Frank Dicksee – *Sir* Frank Dicksee. Here is your 2d back and please accept ten shillings to go with it and thank you for being so kind to a poor old man. I took his ten bob and my 2d. Well I thought he could afford it.

Then he said, A word of sound advice to you, young man: Never lose your friendly nature or goodwill towards men. We shook hands and parted. Only one thing annoyed me about this pleasing incident. I did not ask for his autograph and I can't think why I didn't. I am so sure that he'd obliged me. Might even have drawn a little picture and by a P.R.A. that would have been unique. But to look at him you'd never have thought that he was anyone, he looked like an *has been* actor . . . or artist.

¶ *December 18th 1929*

A wonderfully lucky day of trade. Just when I was miserable and had been in my shop in Camberwell since eight in the morn there came a good fairy at five (and it was raining and miserable outside). The books stood like chorus girls in a row waiting to be picked out and this man did the picking. These are what he bought. *Young Woodley* (the novel), *Santa Claus in Summer* by C. Mackenzie, *St Christopher's Day* by Martin Armstrong, *Hans Frost* by Walpole, *Dodsworth* by Sinclair Lewis, *Odtaa* by Masefield, *Sorell and Son* by Deeping, *The Key of Life* by Brett Young, *The Sailors Return* by David Garnett (said to be a one time bookseller himself) *The King who was a King* by H. G. Wells. Man paid me six shillings each for all of them. They were all first editions and the state was very nice without being exactly mint. Said he was delighted to meet me and the oasis of intelligent books and a man who much loved his wares. He paid cash. He wanted to buy a letter that P. G. Wren had sent me two days ago but of course I refused to part with a letter. They are my hobby and as he was nice I suggested that it would cost just two stamps and some politeness and then I am sure Wren would write to him. That didn't seem to occur to my client. I am reading *The Squeaker* by Edgar Wallace. I didn't show the intelligent client what the intelligent bookman was reading *but* I enjoy a Wallace...so there it is.

¶ *Looking back on the year 1929*

As I grow older I think that I will say that this was one of the very happiest years with me. I went to plays often and the music hall once a week. I got the money for these pleasures by tipping greyhounds that other people bet on and some gave me as gifts around 5 to 15% of their winnings. I did *not* bet more than two dogs a week myself and they were just personal fancies, seldom part of my system of winner finding.

I had a great bit of luck at a first night. It was of a play by dear A. A. Milne called *The Ivory Door*. It was failure of a play and yet was really lovely produced. On the first night I asked Aubrey Hammond for his autograph and instead of giving it he took from his overcoat a sketch of one of the costumes for it drawn in pencil on a piece of handmade paper 7½ by 5 all done by himself and signed it in the corner by him. Man offered me a pound for it right after A. H. had gone in a car. I did not take it and won't ever. It's for my personal library.

A lot of fuss was made this year about *The Apple Cart* by Shaw. I think it was a far too long winded-talkie talkie. But will admit that C. Hardwicke was jolly good (but then I have yet to see him jolly bad). A great actor died this year – Leslie Faber. Such a nice bloke and so intelligent. And Diaghileff the very greatest producer of Ballet passed on. I do wish I'd got his autograph but he refused twice and I did not care to ask again. To beg I'd be ashamed.

If I was asked who made the biggest personal hit of 1929 I would say Gracie Fields. She packed the Victoria Palace. The revue was all Gracie Fields and she was a winner. John Galsworthy came up with another play. This was called *Exiled*. I did not care for it. (I don't pay 5s to be miserable). I would not have seen his other play *The Roof* except that darling Madeleine Carroll was in it and it was worth 3s 6d to gaze at her lovely face. The play did not run long. I was rather lucky at *The Roof* first night for Galsworthy signed for me a rather battered copy of *The Man of Property*. The book cost me fifteen shillings. I resold it for fifty shillings to a bookbinder who said it's to be beautifully rebound and going to America. I sent Mr Galsworthy ten bob out of me profit for his sick animal fund. With the rest I purchased cigarette cards.

¶ *January 3rd 1930*

Ann Penn, the great impersonator gave me and my mum a box at the Alhambra what cost 23s 6d. Said that my faithfull admiration had to be rewarded and that a box at The Alhambra is something I might always remember. I will! I had just seated myself and put me cap on the ledge when me blooming cap fell off said ledge right bang down on the top of a woman's head! She didn't half look daggers. I went and got me cap back and nearly got lost finding me way back to *our box*.

¶ *January 12th*

Enid Stamp Taylor (of the peaches and cream face) got married – to a stockbroker. And I got a quid from her to drink her health. Did her other fans get £1 as well? If so its a good job her old man is rich! The quid came by post with the request to stop what I was doing and go and get a drink . . . and when it came I was just going into the W.C.! I continued my journey!

¶ *January 15th*

Mrs Christie sent me a new and unsigned copy of *Murder on the Links*. That was sweet. But what was *not* sweet was the fact that on this day Seamark, a very grand thriller writer, put his head in gas oven and ended his life. Why? Why?

¶ *January 21st*

Saw the first night of *Journeys End* and what a modest man was R. E. Sheriff. In my opinion a downright real gentleman. By his kind modest manner of signing my book he's made a fan for life.

¶ *February 21st*

I saw Emil Jannings in a great film called *The Last Command* and I must confess, diary, that I cried. This is the first time for years that a film has moved me to tears. I doubt if I will ever see such great film acting as that of Emil Jannings for many years. And Sunday 24th I went to the Albert Hall and heard Kreisler. He's the best fiddler in the world. I paid 6s and got wonderful value. For a pin I could have cried again. What am I getting – a sissy? I was moved with his music. If I confessed this to anyone in Walworth they would laugh at me. Kreisler had ten recalls. Ten times he came out and bowed – bowed as if he knew that he deserved it.

Sunday night at the Strand saw *Rope*. And the Sunday was March the third. I will remember this day as well. I've been giving a girl 10s a week for her bottom drawer – our funds to get married on. I find that she ain't saved a bleedin shilling of it. All spent on her bloke. And she calls me a mug – and that's what I am. But I marked her – her bloke will not fancy her tonight. And I'll mark him as well when I sees him. Seven pounds ten she's had. Here's me 22, fit and well and right ready to get me a home and family and now this. I'll be sure next time. Norman says its a lot better to find out before than afterwards. Seven pounds ten ain't nuffink against the price of a miserable life with the wrong woman.

Him and me went to *Rope* together. The play made me forget, it was that good. Women! Cor luv a duck.

¶ *March 20th*

Love Lies at the Gaiety. *Love Lies!* I am still feeling the twist of that bitch who did me down. Laddie Cliff so very good in this show. I chatted with Arthur Rigby and Phyliss Monkman: both such nice folks, so kind, so human. Arthur was interested in a set of 1901 cigarette cards I showed him. Phyliss gave me the largest signed photo I've yet possessed.

March 29th

I saw a talkie – that's what they call them – talkies 'cause they talk as you sees the film. This one was called *White Shadows of the South*. I saw it at the Rialto. 2s 6d. for a seat but well worth it. Sax Rohmer wrote such a nice letter to me this day so all in all a grand day.

¶ *April 4th*

I purchased 55 copies of *Young Men in Love* by M. Arlen and 67 copies of *Red Sky in the Morning* by

Margaret Kennedy and 15 copies of *Swan Song* by Galsworthy at 1s 6d each copy. I fully expect to sell the lot by next week. These are sellers – not of course in Walworth or on my Barrow – but to Public Libraries all over the country. Ask 2s 6d a copy. I will retain one of each to be signed by the respective authors and put them in my personal library – my 'nest egg'. The money for this gamble came from the sale of 300 rare 'Duke's' cigarette cards.

¶ *April 5th*

John Drinkwater came to my home and spent an hour and a half. I thought he'd talk poems and plays but *all* that he spoke about was STAMP COLLECTING. Blime! But he autographed 5 of his books for me.

¶ *April 10th*

This night at His Majesty's theatre (*Porgy*) I saw for the first time Lord Beaverbrook, but he looks just like anyone else. I did not ask for his autograph but did ask and got H. G. Wells.

June the 25th was a remarkable day for I had nice letters from G. K. Chesterton and Elinor Glyn and could there be two such contrasts in the world of letters? Both wanted copies of their own first editions, three G.K.C. and four novels Elinor. This is the result of a write up about me – that I liked to sell to authors their own early novels and feel that the books are going to the right homes when they return to their writers after many years. Today I read a nice novel by Herbert Asquith called *Young Orland*. Surely this man is a winner for first edition stakes in the future?

¶ *June 30th*

I saw *Broadway Melody*, this is the best talkie I've yet seen. Every bit of it was enjoyable.

In the evening I went to tea with Mrs Belloc Lowndes, a dear old lady, so chatty. But she has got Cats – siamese ones – and there was me balancing a cup on one knee and a plate of nice cakes on the other knee and there was the bloody cats pawing at my legs and digging their claws right through me trousers, and me wanting to kick them cats out of the way – and me listening to small talk from Mrs Lowndes and feeling proper in pain from them claws. Then to hell. I gets up. I puts down the tea cup and then the plate of cakes. I gets me up. I gets hold of one cat, I grabs at the other, misses it (still holding the other very firmly) I misses and trips over a tiny Victorian table what goes over. I grabs again at the cat and gets it this time. I have two cats by the scruff of their smokey colour necks. I don't say a blind word. I goes to the door and clasping one of them to me chest I opens the door and I throws 'em *both* outside. I comes back and picks up the little table, then I sits me down, picks up my tea cup and the eats and says, *You were saying?* and Mrs Belloc Lowndes is such a nice old lady that she continued about Queen Victoria and her doings like as if nothing had happened. But just as I left her I did say, 'Under me trousers is me skin. I can stand somethings but I do not care to be clawed by cats –

not even if they are showing their pleasure' and I leaves it at that.

On July the 1st I purchases 15 copies of *The Miracle Boy* by Louis Golding. I think they are a worth while investment at paying 2s 6d each for fine ex lib, for this is a boxing novel and well written. I do not know if Golding will ever be collected but I am sure that *The Miracle Boy* will be wanted as the years go on. On the other hand I sold nine copies of *King who was a King* by H. G. Wells today at 3s 6d, making a profit of 6d on each copy. I was so glad to get rid of them. This is a poor novel. Yes, 9 copies to one man. He is trying to corner the Wells market. He'll drown in that b— well.

¶ *July 10th*

I was at B.B.C. when H. G. Wells was talking and we had five minutes conversation. He said he liked *Mr Polly* of all his books and added that to be remembered by that novel alone would please him. Amiable mood. Made no bones about signing my album. (Actually for the 2nd time – but his is a swopable autograph.)

¶ *August 29th*

My birthday. I got miserable – not a soul in the whole world sent me a card of greeting and I did not get a gift. So I went out and had two wiskeys called doubles and they were nasty taste and I felt sick and wished I had not had them. I came home and tried to read *Go She Must* by David Garnett, but it was meself that went – to sleep.

¶ *September 15th*

This day I saw Gloria Swanson in *The Trespasser*, the third talkie I've witnessed and the best of the three.

¶ *September 18th*

Saw The *Calender* by E. Wallace, a really grand play … and witnessed Fame in a gracefull manner for this night Edgar Wallace signed at the very least fifty albums and 50 programmes and gave a kind word to each and all and nothing put him out. Here is a *nice* celebrity.

¶ *September 22nd*

I went for the first time ever to The Bermondsey Bookshop where they try so hard to hold up the flag of good literature in the slums. All were so very nice to me. H. W. Nevinson was charming. A lovely small company of real booklovers. I felt so very much at home.

¶ *October 7th*

I sold the autograph of Sir Oliver Lodge for the sum of 12s 6d. Its the very first time I have sold an autograph, but truly, diary, I did not want it, and I did need 12s 6d to buy cigarette cards with.

¶ *October 15th*

All people seem to want is *All Quiet on the Western Front*. I ain't got it and don't want it.

On October the 20th I went to the Gallery First Nighters club (after the afternoon with Tetrazainni the singer) and found nice Ashley Dukes there. This night read a new author, E. Sackville West. O.K. All in all a lovely year. When I reckons up after all paid I will have made 15 pounds and 50 pals. Would like to make 5000 friends by the time I'm 50.

¶ *March 3rd 1931*

Tonight at Foyles Mr Alfred Noyes who is a poet-bloke will read the works of Mr Alfred Noyes – which is alright for Mr Noyes for the noise that he will make will be his own music and he will get paid for it and likely sell some of the copies of the books from which he quotes. I do wonder if the day will ever arrive when Foyles will ask me to read extracts from some of my writings. Indeed if they ask me I am very sure that I shall faint from sheer amazement – but *only* after I know what they are going to *pay* me.

But seriously I do think it's a good idea for poets and writers to be invited to read from their own writings and be seen. Shows that they are mortal man just like anyone else, although some of the writers of 1931 seem very precious lads and extreemly arty arty. I have a wish to hear Robert Service read *The Green Eye of the little Yellow God*. Indeed, if anyone had the slightest sense they'd get him to make a gramaphone record of it. And some of Aldous Huxley's wisdom would be well on a record. Much as I dislike Kipling I think if he said his poem *If* for a gramaphone company it would be an o.k.

seller. In fact I wish right now to copyright a really original
and brainwave of an idea. *Short Stories by Famous Authors*
read by their authors on a series of gramaphone records
for Public libraries all over the country so that they can
be interchanged. Maugham telling us one of his short
shorts. Edgar Wallace giving us a thrill. Even me speaking
in real Cockney a couple of real London tales, so that when
I am dead they will be able to say, well, he was at least a
real Londoner, you can hear it in his speech. And why
not a sporting series of records? My greatest fight, by
Carpentier?

¶ *January 9th 1931*

Madeleine Carroll has this day sent a postcard asking
me to send her my latest attempt at playwriting called
Guests Without Chaperons. And, my golly, I cannot. This
play is rather a sort of *Liza of Lambeth* or rather 'Winnie
of Walworth' and she is a whore and this three act play
is about her loves. Maugham has done me the kindness
of reading it and said nice kind things of it *but* I must
refuse to send it to sweet Madeleine. Diary, you know
what happened to me? I was alone in my attic. Was a girl-
hungry bloke: had a sexy urge on me and to sort of get
it out of me system I wrote this play, like others (I am
told) write flaming novels. Bert says it's a fair play but
has raw edges and I will be very wise to wait.

All in all this is going to be the *bestest* yet year of my
life, this 1931. Five months time my book on Maugham
and his writings will be on the market. Each week for
months now Maugham has sent to me postcards from

where ever he happens to be and now I have 87 cards from him, all with neat comments on the places viewed upon the other side of the cards. The one yesterday from Egypt just says: 'MY...its 'ot. W.S.M.'

Maugham is a funny bloke. I do not know what on earth he wants from *me* but he's real pally. Maybe he thinks that I shall make the grade some-day and that his mantle will fall on me. But I don't want a *cast off* mantle. If I make any grade I want it to be on me own and off me own bat. Right in front of me is a chance to be a playwriter, for I am pretty sure Madeleine don't write unless she is genuine keen to see and get others to see my play, *but* I am *ashamed* of it. Some day I shall do better. Have a lovely plot for a play called *Three Ladies in Black*. Will tell Miss Carroll that I do not consider the play worthy of her.

¶ *June 1st 1931*

I treated myself to a seat in the circle tonight to see again the wonderfull Ruth Draper at The Vaudeville Theatre and have supper afterwards all posh in Soho. This was a luxury and I had to save up quite a time to get the money for this do, but it does me good. Makes a change.

Tomorrow I start out in a new line and richer as well because my publishers are going to give me Five pounds advance royalities on my Somerset Maugham Bibliography and its likely that by the time its all sold out I shall have made fifty pounds and the skies are bright.

I've been having a hell of a time. Up, Down. Thats a bookman's life. But its *my* life. Tomorrow at my book-shop I may take five pounds or not even fivepence. Never know. All this has one disadvantage. Lack of security. Can't very well ask a girl to share my life. Likely as not I shall never marry. I have never really known security. My mother in a fit of temper could turn me out of home at any time. If it wasn't for my dear dad home life would not be very pleasant. Family life...Home...My God! ...A lonely room and my loyal and trusted pals mostly good books on the walls. A few signed photos of pretty ladies, none who'd care if I was starving. Home... I hear parties next door so often. Ain't been a party in my home in years and years. Home. But that's the tragedy of being an only son forty years younger than your people. You don't grow up *with* them. Yours is another world.

¶ *1931*

I was on my way to buy some books from a lady at Notting Hill. As I was walking down the street behind the tube station I saw a little girl with a big doll. Passing without speaking did not seem right, so I stopped and said, 'You've got a lovely dolly...What is the name of your dolly, little girl?' And the child replied...'Hush... don't let my baby know that she is only a Dolly.' So I hushed – and passed on.

¶ *January 1934*

I've been pretty busy over this Christmas season what with one thing and another. I had a little job of playing the piano to tide over the bad season and I got 15s a night and that was very nice. But the job has ceased now and I can return to my new selling line, cigarette card sets.

I have to record the death of Eugene Corri the boxing ref, who looked like a tough sergeant major and acted like one and when he said 'BREAK!' God help the boxer who didn't do it. He seldom got another job if Gene had his way. I would put him down as one of the most colourfull personalities of the ring in past fifty years, but I have heard more boxers say they hated his guts than any other ref or man in the game. His dad was an Irish baritone in the Carl Rosa Opera company and his real name was *Corry* ...he changed it to *Corri* for the snobbish reason of the Italian sound of it.

Corri was a Bohemian and went from the top to the bottom of life. It was only last year that he published *Fifty Years in the Ring,* which is a good boxing work and the sort that all fight fans should have. He had a very poor opinion of Boxers and their Brainwork. He was the sort of bloke who knew everybody and made sure that everybody knew him. But he did do a lot of good in the Ring for he would never never have any messing around when he was ref. The boxers were paid to fight and by Heck they'd fight and be damned to them. He was a giant in the fight world in the late 1890s but when he died at 76 on December the 20th he was but a memory. He lived at Southend and probably died broke.

¶ *Christmas Day 1936*

Perhaps the nicest surprise of this Christmas has been an unexpected letter from Robert Hichens. It comes from

a place called *Ain Shams* near Cairo on the edge of the
desert. I think it's Ain shame that I am not with him instead
of shivering here in London. He raised a point about *The
Green Carnation* which I recently wrote about in one of
my American book articles. Says that as the book was
written forty years ago he is very very tired of it and
would prefer to be remembered for *Bella Donna* rather
than for a Carnation. He says that it served its purpose.
Of course it did, Mr Hichens. It made you famous almost
in a week and but for it you might never have gone from
strength to strength and made a tidy fortune so that you
can winter in Egypt or anywhere else you choose! You
ought to put flowers on Oscar Wilde's dismal grave once
a year in thanks. No Wilde: no carnation!

¶ *March 1937*

The death of John Drinkwater has left a gap in my life,
like the turning of a page, for it was through him or his
advice that I came to know in turn Stephen Graham,
Arnold Bennet, John Galsworthy and others. He sort of
set the boat swimming down the stream for me in a river
that was almost unknown. He was a dear kind man and
the autographs' collectors' delight. He signed his books
for me on many occasions and I got 3s 6d to 5s more for
them that way than I'd have got unsigned and he *knew*
it. I've got 4 of his signed I'll never sell.

There is little doubt that *Abraham Lincoln* was his finest
play and he told me that it came into its own and did
well for him solely out of the curiousity of the play-going
public. The play was doing badly and likely to come off

at any moment, for the star was very unwell. John stepped into the leading role as a desperate measure to try to save the play, although he admitted that he was nowhere as good as the star or for that matter a good actor at all. He felt that the public came out of sheer curiosity to see if he tripped up. And at times he *did* trip up, just to oblige them. The theatre became packed houses and he was made. He was to me a good kind man and I am now going to buy a black tie and I shall wear it for a whole month in memory of him. I went twice to tea with him and Daisy Kennedy and saw the children. All made me so welcome. a kindly man – who didn't like Hugh Walpole or Maugham. Probably had good reason but never told me the reason, merely the bald statement.

In Whitehall I saw a boy aged about eleven. He was staring at the Horse Guards in an awestruck manner. 'Are you going to be a soldier when you grow up?' I asked him, and after a bit of thought he replied, 'No mister, no'. 'Well, what do you want to be then?' 'I'd like to be Rita Hayworth's manager – she's a smasher.'

I think that even Rita Hayworth, who could manage most men, would find herself with a real job managing this little fellow when he grows up. And it came out pat, like as if he'd given it much thought. Amused me no end. I gave him sixpence.

¶ *December 1937*

No time yet have I been a Kipling fan, although I admit that a few of his books are just readable. We can very well get along without each other. Today however I saw the film *Wee Willie Winkie*. Its a 20th Cent. Fox production based on 'Kip's' tale. It was quite delightful. Has in it a dear little girl named Shirley Temple, who looked sweet enough to eat. It's the first time I have seen this young lady ... reckon she cannot be much more than 10. All the cast was good. Victor McLagen (he once fought Jack Johnson – and of course *lost*) was in smashing form and dear kind C. Aubrey Smith upheld the B. Empire as usual. Noticed such a good looking man name *Cesar Romero*. With such a name how could he possibly fail to become a film star? Or for that matter with such a smile and grand teeth, the girls will go for him. Also in the cast is *June Lang*, who I think is very attractive and again not ever seen in a film before. I forget who directed this nice film but even disagreeable 'Kip' would I think be pleased with this 'Willie'. Shirley Temple is really clever ... and Loveable. P.S. There are some tales in *Plain Tales from the Hills* which would be filmable, also *Soldiers Three* would make a mighty film.

¶ *May 1938*

Looking back, I don't think so much ever happened to me in one week that was so pleasant . . . and indeed profitable as well. I was at B.B.C. rehearsing for a 15 minute talk on the art of collecting cigarette cards when a bloke there said I have a few books, when you've done this job perhaps you'd care to come round the corner to my flat. I went. A few books was over a hundred. He asked five pounds the lot. I paid him five pounds right there and then.

I had 4s 6d left. I called a cab, I put them all in the cab and in less than 30 minutes I'd sold the lot for fifty five shillings clear profit. They were all novels of the Austin Freeman-Sapper variety and I had no trouble to sell them. Then I broadcasts at 3.45 – 15 minutes. 4 o'clock had the bellyache bad. I like the wages but the job gives me butterflies in the belly.

That same day I met for the first time in person L. A. G. Strong. He autographed nine copies of his novels – not all different ones, just all that I had collected. I do not think I shall sell these for some years. He is a writer with a future and I will gamble on that future, with nine to start me off. On B.B.C. for 15 minutes. I got ten guineas. But the 55/- in between rehersal and talk pleased me most.

But the next day was the day – dozens and dozens of letters, all from folks who heard my talk on the radio and wanted odd cards to complete their sets. I've often sold complete sets but now I have a ready made business come right to my door. I will supply odd cards to the folks who need a few cards to make their sets complete. I have nearly two million cards. There is very little I cannot supply. Trade generally speaking has been poor and I think that its wise to have this side line. Writing is alright but I only intend all my life, to write facts in the first person, and so the longer I live the more I shall have interesting facts. It's cards for me from now onwards. I am a cigarette card dealer. (Wonder if anyone else has ever got a business founded *solely* on a 15 minutes B.B.C. talk?)

Next day I made a film... well, I started it this day and finished on the Friday for Ace Films in Abbey Street. It was me showing the wide variety of cigarette cards for a

magazine feature. This also came from the little B.B.C. talk.
Enterprising firm. Hear talk and next afternoon fix up to
make film the next afternoon. I do four hours that day
and two hours the next morning. I am paid two pounds
for the job. I wonder what Greta Garbo gets or for that
matter James Mason for a film. I do know that the young
chap who they call the clapper boy (scene one, take three)
got twice my wages per week. But what matter? It's all
experience and one must pay for that. They said I was
very easy to film.

Well, there I was with 10 gns from B.B.C. and 2 quid
from Ace Film company. What did I do? I packed my
week-end case on the Saturday morning, said ta ta and I
did not know when I'd be back, and off I went first by train
to Brighton and then right along the South coast, a day
here, a bus onwards, a day there, a night here, early
morning off to there . . . on and on. Brighton, Seaford,
Eastbourne, St Leonards, Hastings, Rye, New Romney,
Folkestone, Dover, Deal, Sandwich, Ramsgate, Margate,
and it was there at Margate that I found that I had just
enough money for one good meal and my fare back home.
So I had the good meal – and went back home to answer
mail from B.B.C.

This was something that I had for years and years wanted
to do, and as it affected no one but me I did it. I now want
to go from Brighton to Portsmouth or even Southampton,
just suiting myself how long I stay in each place and
moving on to just where I want to go. I cannot think of
a nicer way to spend money. Had no adventures whatever.
No one did me down and there was no romance en route
but it was all a very lovely time.

After all, to do what you'd set your heart on doing, and taken around ten years to be able to do it, well that is Something. No one can take away the memory of that lovely holiday. I shall remember it all my life. Of the places, Eastbourne was the nicest. But for a real good meal at a fair price Brighton was the place. Folkestone was so dull and why ever anyone goes to Dover save to cross to France, I have no idea. Rye had charm. The times I'd promised myself this trip! Well I've done it and I am a very satisfied bloke. As I sort out cigarette cards I shall remember Beachy Head. As the children scream in the streets I shall recall the romance of Rye.

¶ *15th July 1938*

This day was pleasant because L. A. G. Strong came to tea and autographed six more books of his to me. I have been putting these aside since May when I went to his place for tea. He is a gentleman. There is no doubt about that and he is a good friend of mine. He's not a man who laughs easily but when he does, it's a lovely laugh. And he laughed five times this evening. I believe that the day will arrive when collectors of first editions will collect the novels of L. and so I will put these aside and then, when I am famous and L. is more famous, I will sell them. Oh yes, I will sell them, for Leonard has said thats what I *must* do! But I won't do so for years yet.

¶ *December 1938*

I feel that this must be recorded. Today I received Twelve Christmas cards all from One American lady

who's a fan of mine. Ruth lives in New York City. Last
August she sent to me her photo and I would guess that
she is all of seventeen stone (I'm eight). It's been said that
small men adore large women. But NOT all this large *in
my* case. The cards sent by Ruth bear ONE word on each
card: These - are - to - wish - you - a - very - Happy
Christmas - Freddie - from - Ruth . . . and after the 12
envelopes and their cards (all sealed down) came a short
letter by the next post to say that she was unable to chose
the best from the 12, so she sent the 12. And these, with
one from ever-faithfull Lizzie, were all the cards I had
this as usual lonely Christmas.

I spent Christmas day reading *Jess* by Haggard and
Green Mantle by J. Buchan. They were books I'd put
aside for personal reading when I had the chance and at
Christmas there was the chance. I tried to talk to my
mother but gave it up when she said that my speaking
stopped her writing her correspondence. My dad sleeped
most of the day – with his head on one chair and his feet
on another and his slim body sagging in the middle with
no support. I don't know how he ever gets to sleep like
this; but he does, and has done it for years, although we
HAVE got a bed. I dread Christmas and if I ever get a bit
rich I will book myself a hotel on the south coast and get
me far far from London at this time of the year where
there might be a party. My God, a party! I ain't never
had a Xmas party in me own home. I have a tinge of what
they call self pity this Christmas and wish even the large
size Ruth was here. I shall be happy when this day has
passed.

Have you got a spicy book young man?

What, mam, at Your age?

Whatyer mean my age? you ain't never too old for spice.
I was a Gaiety girl before you was even thought of . . .
Spice . . . once you've had it . . . you don't want to do
without it. My age indeed. I am only 71. Confound your
cheek . . . and off she went.

From that day onwards I let the old girls chose their
own poison and never made any comment, for I found
that lost me a customer, that bit of impudence. I learnt me
lesson from that old girl, never to argue, the customer is
right . . . because They pay the bill.

¶ *Heard in Brixton, 1939, outside The Empress Music Hall*

> *I'm very poor. Oh Lor Lummy,*
> *I'm very poor – got no money.*
> *Got some kids and gotta wife,*
> *Oh Lor Lummy, what a life!*

This was sung by a middle-aged man who was very
stout. He wore a ladies hat and a ladies spring coat. He
said after this song, 'Thats all there is in that one'. He
called it his signature tune – but was *unable* to write his
own name! His repetoire consists of this, *Sweet Adeline*
and *Old Folks at Home*. This above ditty was sung *between
each song*. The whole performance took less than ten
minutes – then he passed around of his ladies hat. A move
up the street and off we go again:

I'm very poor. Oh Lor Lummy,
I'm very poor – got no money.
Got some kids and gotta wife,
Oh Lor Lummy, what a life!

What a life! He considered it a very *poor* week if he did not take £3 10s od in pennies.

¶ *Heard in Lambeth, 1942*

This little song was sung by a Cockney mother to her baby in a pram beside an old clothes stall in a Lambeth market. She said she'd made it up – and used it on four children and this was her fifth – and nicest, so far.

Go to sleep you little beggar
Go to sleep – Don't mind the weather.
Whether it rains or whether it's dry
You'll pay taxes till you die!
Go to sleep you little lamb
Nothing's gonna hurt my little man,
Take a kip now while you may
Tomorrow's a blooming long way away
Go to sleep, sleep, sleep.

The song certainly did the trick, for her fifth was very soon fast asleep. It could have been the song – or could have been that the baby was tired out!

¶ *1943*

Tonight I sat in Hyde Park. It's August and the weather is fine. Myself I was alone with a novel by Richmal Crompton, but very close to me was a young couple. They were kissing and cuddling, enjoying every minute of their blissfull moments. I didn't watch them. If I'd had a woman right then I'd have done much the same thing. As the darkness deepened and I was not able to see the words of the novel I did nothing and doing nothing is often very pleasant. I looked at the reflections of the sky on the Serpentine and listened to the birds. It could well have been deep in the heart of the country. All was very pleasant.

Then there came down the path beside the lake the heavy tread of either a soldier or a copper. I looked up. It was a copper and so I just looked down at the water again. The steps slowed as this person came to the seat of the lovers – went by – came back. For a moment there was silence and then the copper said, 'Better move on'. A man's voice said, 'Why? We are doing no harm!' Copper said, 'Don't say WHY to ME. Move on when I tell you to. Break it up. Love-making in Public. Go on – clear off.' Footsteps were heard. I could not see them although they were not far away. The lovers came my way. The girl said, 'Where CAN we go?' The man said that the policeman was a swine.

I felt down right sorry for them lovers. Very probably they had nowhere else to go, except a dark alley. I do think that the police might use a scrap of discretion and commonsense if they have such things. They probally once made love themselves. It seems to me that a great many people in England right now need to know how to Love and realise that there is nothing shamefull in loving. Too often the official side of London seems to

C

think that its shamefull for human beings to take their love together. No one wants sheer beastliness in Hyde Park, but those two were just kissing and teaseing and having quiet fun and there was not a soul near but me, and I didn't mind a bit.

¶ *January 1st 1945*

Tonight I treated Lizzie and myself to extra nice seats to see Sid Field in *Strike It Again*. Field was just as amusing as he was in the days at the South London Music hall long before he was discovered. Like a good many clever comics, he'd been round and round the halls for years without setting the Thames on fire, then he gets a break and does the *same* things in the same way at five time more salary and his name in lights at The Prince of Wales Theatre. Lizzie enjoyed the show and I enjoyed the very attractive lot of show girls.

This day, as trade has been so bad, I have applied to the Ministry of Education for a job as a maker of original toys for children out of things which cost nothing (I can make 200 good toys from worthless oddments. They are appealing for teachers and I am very sure that I can hold a class room of children as I show them how to make toys for nothing). (I have already written two books on the subject.)

Tomorrow I lunch at The Café Royal for the first time in my life. I am the guest of Eric Hiscock of the *Evening Standard*. He pays the bill and I am to answer all his questions so that he can write a profile on me for a mag. called *Pie*. He will get about ten gns for his profile. I will eat ten bobs worth of food plus the thrill of going where James Agate so often went, and so Eric will be the winner; at least I hope so, for he's a very nice man.

¶ *Saturday 13th January 1945*

This was a rather sad day because from now onwards I've got to wear glasses for reading – indeed I can no longer read without them. They cost me 16s 9d and the Panel allowed 12s 6d towards the cost. I am told that they make me look intelligent and becoming to a literary man but by golly I would sooner be going and not to have them.

¶ *Tuesday 8th May 1945*

This is v.e. Day and the war is over. Peace at last. I ought to report here that I had a great day but I did nothing except have two double whiskeys with Lizzie and then go out and get the autograph of Randolph Sutton, who has been on the halls for around thirty years and I thought it was about time I got me round to asking him. That's all I did. He was very amiable and we had another whiskey and three Wiskeys always set me back, so I was very care-full how I walked down the road in case I fell over and couldn't get up. I got me home alright, laid straight on the bed and had a very lovely long dreamless sleep. When I got up, I said a prayer for thanks to God for sparing Lizzie and me, so that I could write more to make the world smile and Liz could give me fans tea and cakes when they called upon me on Thursdays. Thursday is always my AT HOME day to everyone. Being early closing day it's the only day there's a little silence in Walworth.

¶ *1945*

It is a very lovely summers afternoon and I have the deck chair (I bought for 3s 6d on Christmas Eve) on the bit of a lawn, which is the size of an average dining room table. I am reading *Esquire* which my fan Gene in Los Angeles has sent to me that very day – I am very happy with the world. I am even singing. I sing *Come into the garden Maud*. Liz comes to me chair and she says 'That is a very old song which you are a trying to sing. Do you know who wrote it?' I thinks, and then I says that I am pretty sure that the words at least were written by Tennyson – Lord Tennyson. She thinks a moment – and Liz does have her moments – and then she says, 'He must be getting to be a very old man now. I heard that song when I was young as well!' I agree that he must be a very old man. She then says, 'Have you got his autograph?' I have to say that I haven't. 'Then hadn't you better set about it right now? People don't last for ever, Lords *especially*. He'll be dead and then you'll be sorry that you missed him and he'll be nice to go along side Irving Berlin, won't he?' I agree that side by side they would be smashing. She goes in very cheerfull and I return to *Esquire:* but its not half so funny as my Lizzie.

¶ *February 1946*

Been told a lovely tale. Entirely true and it's got a moral I think, although I can't put me finger on it.

In the front of a South Coast hotel there were wicker chairs for the residents and in one of them was an ex-lightweight boxing champion.

(He told me this tale against himself.) He has a tin ear and scars of his trade, and although he's now pretty nearly fifty-five he's a well set up and active bloke. A young woman aged no more than twenty-one got fascinated in him and tried all ways to get very friendly with him. Now his wife did not care who he went around with or even slept with so long as he was round when she was in the mood and so long as she got her weekly wage packet.

I'm going to call this bloke Bob (it's not his name). He was quite willing for a pleasant little interlude of flirtation with not much harm done and very soon they got to chatting and then going for little walks and the girl got a real kick out of being seen around on the arm of the ex-pug – although he was old enough to be her father. One evening she very calmly suggested that she was quite willing to share his bed one night for the fun of it. After all they were both on holiday and no one need never never know. She could so easily slip into his room one night for an hour or so, her room being just above his, and the bathroom on the landing outside his room. It was all so easy.

Bob was an ordinary bloke, the girl was attractive. It was obvious that the girl was no innocent. She boasted of several American GIs to her credit. So Bob agreed to leaving his door open at eleven that very night so that she could slip into the room and into his bed. It didn't seem a bit sordid, the way Bob told it, just nicely romantic. He made no preparations, just an extra close shave and an extra good bath. He was reading *Boxing News* when she came in. He looked at her. She had a thin dressing gown on and apart from that was nude.

He said that he saw that she had a mole on her chest

and he opened his mouth to comment upon it, when she gave a gasp and said out loud, 'NO...NO' and ran from the room. He was absolutely astounded. He got up from bed and looked at himself in the glass. *He'd forgotten to put in his teeth.* He made some remark to the mirror and the sight shocked him – the toothless leer of a battered old pug. He returned to bed, put out the light and had a vivid dream of the young miss who got a thrill out of being in the company of a one time Boxing champion.

In the morning he paid his bill and left the hotel without seeing the girl. He said that he never wants to see her again or have flirtations with women thirty years his junior, said that a woman over thirty would not have minded. 'Damn it all, I didn't want to *eat* the blooming girl!' But he said that forever afterwards he was very careful about having his teeth in when his old woman wanted a bit of loving.

¶ *June 9th 1947*

Today there was a memorial service at St Martins-in-the-Fields for James Agate, and I was present. I only put on a black tie because I was pretty sure Agate would have been proper annoyed if I'd have gone and brought a black cap especially for the occasion. I would not buy a black trilby again because for some reason every time I wears a black trilby I get mistaken for Arthur Helliwell of *The People*. Twice I had to show my identity-card plus some letters to prove that I am me. And I rather think that I escaped a good beating up on one of these occasions by three angry men in Wardour Street who took a lot of proof before they would believe that I was me and not

Arthur, although in height we are as Mutt and Jeff. In looks we are very much alike. He could easily be my big brother.

The memorial service was well attended and by people who I am sure were not all his friends whilst he lived. And everyone spoke so well of him and how sadly he will be missed, some who didn't care a dam for him when alive and spoke unkindly of him so often. Do you have always to wait untill you are dead in order to get friendly words from colleagues? James Agate was several times kind to me and I shall miss him and the little short chats we had from time to time, but most of all I shall miss him for seeing that he put me on the road to fame by telling me to keep a diary and some day it will keep me.

¶ *August 29th 1947*

Today is my birthday. In the year which has passed I have received eight hundred and forty two letters which can honestly be called fan mail, since for the most part these kind folks only wanted to let me know how much my writings have been enjoyed by them. All were complete strangers to me. Not a single relation has *ever* congratulated me in any way at any time. How true was Arnold Bennett's words that you do not get praise from your nearest and dearest.

I have answered every one of these letters even when they really didn't need a reply. Put it down to goodwill and international friendship. When no one bothers to write to me, I shall know my days in the world of letters are over. I would say that from this 800 odd letters I have made four friends. That's nice ... and a good average. I also got twenty-three girls offering their hearts or something. Today ever faithfull Lizzie gave me two winter shirts for my birthday gift. I was most obliged. Poor dear, why cannot I ever remember her birthday? I don't, it always slips by. I feel so ashamed when the day after she gently reminds me what yesterday was. These shirts are extra long ones she had made for me and go right down to me knees and will keep me little bottom very warm this winter.

¶ *December 1947*

There is a scene in *Forlorn Sunset* by Michael Sadleir that was so real in my own life. It's on page 296 where Arthur is pleading with Hetty and we can realise only too well his love for her and see so clearly what she is missing by not saying 'yes'. This happened to me with a girl named Katherine. Oh how dearly I loved her. She'd been my heart's delight for several years and I'd skimped and saved just so that I had enough money to buy a nice home for her. I adored her. She was class with a big C. I proposed to her one afternoon and Lizzie who knew what K. meant and of my dreams left us alone all of an hour – and God how I begged K. to marry me. With her by my side I'd have climbed to the top! But she said 'no'. She was going to pray for the sins of the world and do missionary work! I tried so hard. I broke down. She went. I never saw her again. I was ill for five weeks. Between life and death I didn't want to live. The colour had gone from life. The reason for working had gone with no Katherine. There was nothing. But it's funny – a broken heart does mend. I haven't seen her for two or three years – but I shall never quite forget her. She was colder than marble. Beautifull to look upon. But she had no warmth – at least not for me! And I learnt later that she'd jilted one man right on the altar steps. Changed her mind three minutes before Yes! It was all for the best for me.

¶ *At my barrow of books these things happened. (1947?)*

She was a rather attractive girl. Her age would be around twenty. She stood awhile sorting over the books on the better side of my barrow, where the better editions of better literature stood in rows. She did not seem to know what to choose, so I asked if I could help her. And she explained her need. 'I want a learned looking book. You know, something what looks serious. I am meeting my new chap tonight and he's rather a stick in the mud (dud) at the little things a girl likes, so I want to sort of impress him...like...No, I don't want to *read* it – only carry it. You can tell me a bit about what it's about. Then when he sees that I am serious as well and the evening gets boring like, he might thor out. Anyrate I thinks, it's worth the chance.' So I sold her an impressive edition of Gibbon's *Decline and Fall of the Roman Empire*, well bound and in perfect state, for a shilling. I said that the title tells the whole tale and he'll be impressed alright.

It was all of a week later. The young woman passed my barrow – and I have a good memory for faces – and as trade was poor I touched me cap in complete politeness and asked how she had got on with *Decline and Fall* and if it had worked the trick. Had he been impressed with her serious reading? She said, No, it hadn't been at all a success. 'He seemed pleased to see the book under me arm and then he started asking me all silly questions about it. I tried to evade 'em, but I soon got caught out and then I got angry with him and...Well, I left the blooming book with him. Don't ever want to see him any more. Got a new bloke. He's alright. He's lent me *Forever Amber* and he can *jive*...' and off she went.

'I want a book, mate. For a penny – or no more than tuppence anyway. I want it this size' – and he brings out a grubby bit of newspaper. I have a penny book box. I goes through it and I finds a book that's exactly the height but is a scrap under a quarter of an inch wider than the paper. I shows it to him and he thinks as how it will do. It's a penny and he pays me it with out looking at the title (by Charles Spurgeon, it was). Then he tears off the covers and hands me back the actual book. 'Give that to someone, mate. Me, I dont ever read – can't, no schooling,' he says. 'Then what on earth do you want that book for?' I asks. 'What, these covers? To bung in a window. Window's broken – no glass. Ordinary paper still let's in the draught. These covers will be stouter and warmer and the wind won't blow 'em out. Ta ta.' And off he goes.

¶ *My favourite Cockney story*

Two little boys from London were at the seaside for the first time in their lives and were gazing at the sea. One boy said to the other, 'Cor – ain't there a lot of water!' and the other said, 'You ain't seen nuffink yet – there is *more* water underneath it!'

¶ *May 1948*

A woman asked to be friends with me. We met. She was extremely plain, but I've never been a one for glamour girls and her plainness did not disturb me. We walked in Hyde Park after a meal and she started strait away on getting married.

I asked her point blank why was she so bloody keen on marriage? And she said that I would remember in her mail her writing that she lived in the top room of a six story building? She said I'd remember her telling me also in a letter that her heart was not very good and that she had veins in her legs. I said, yes, I recollect these facts. 'Well?', she said, 'Well, I find it a great task to carry coals up the stairs to my room and no coal man will take it up and I have a shed in the garden and in my state of health I *must* have fires and I find it a great strain on my heart and on my legs as well to carry the coal upstairs – *so I want to get married – see?*

¶ *July 1948*

Amongst my mail last month came a letter from a lady who said that she was very lonely and would like to be friends with me. I was rather intrigued. I had nothing to lose and so I suggested a meeting place so that we could at least look each other over, have a nice meal and a pleasant chat – providing that it did not bind us to further meetings or any obligation. I suggested outside the Haymarket Theatre at seven and I would carry a magazine and wear a checked cap. She replies by return that place and time was o.k. and she'd seen my photo so many times in mags that I need not carry a mag.

Well, diary, we met. She was twenty-nine. She wore a green jumper which displayed a full bust. She had solid almost thick set legs – what one calls 'a sturdy filly'. She had an ordinary and unattractive voice. Put her down as a rather plain working class woman with working class hands. Put her down as a woman just a little fed up with being alone in digs and wanting to do something about it – and not particularly choosey who to do it with – any port in the storm of loneliness.

She was not there on time. She kept me waiting ten minutes and I was just leaving – thinking she'd got the wind up – when the wind brought her up. She apologised for keeping me waiting, saying that she'd been shopping and had gone to much trouble choosing what to wear for this special occasion. I looked her over and I couldn't see anything particularly new or attractive in her tweed skirt, green jumper and woollen hat (sort you mostly see in the Swiss Alps). I assumed it would all come out in the wash and politely said she should not have gone to any expense on my account as it was only a dinner date in a second class Soho restaurant. She looked staggered and then disappointed. I was curious. I said, 'Well, what on earth *have* you bought for this occasion?' And cool and collected she said, 'I bought the daintyest *night-gown* you've ever seen! Its a proper dream!'

I was absolutely astounded. 'Did you say *nightgown?*' 'Oh of course, dear,' she replied. 'But – but I clearly said this was a *dinner* date and a chat so as to get to know something about ourselves!' 'I *know* that. I know *that.*

But I read *between* the lines. I realised you couldn't put on paper exactly what you wanted! I said to myself, I *must* be at my very best for Mr Freddie – so I've bought this lovely night-gown – it got pretty flowers and real lace. *You'll love it*.' But I didn't love it. I didn't see it. I left her right there and then.

Somehow I feel I did the right thing – right for *me!*

¶ *1948*

After a war there are always a lot of recollections and exposures by v.i.p.s and others. I hate war (*not* everyone does, for the old men who always seem to govern never go to war and always seem to come out of wars with a lot of medals which their dear old pals given 'em in the share out, and a great deal more money than they had when war started) and in my writings I have wherever possible avoided mention of war. But I have one war time recollection that I feel is well worth recording because it's a pen picture of The Old Town Crier, Alexander Woollcott himself, whom I only saw once.

The Great Alec was a touchy old so and so and full of his own importance; but when a large bit of American egoism meets a small piece of Cockney egoism then it's the little bit which wins and it was a sheer waste of Woollcott's breath to try to impress me. Actually he did nothing of the sort. He was in a nice kind mood and really very amiable.

I met him during the early part of the war. He was in a restaurant in Soho and I'd been taken there for a meal by a well known actress. They met, they talked a great deal. I minded my own business. Suddenly the big tummy turned around my way and Alec said 'Waal – what do you want out of life?' And he stared at me through glasses like a very old owl. I was going to say peace and quiet, as I'd only just come off twelve hours warden duty after a bad night of raids. I thought a moment. Well, it was no use making a senseless answer to a civil question. I said, 'Waal' (moking his talk best able), 'Waal, I kinder guess a brand new *egg* and a fighting photo of Jack Dempsey would please me right now.' The actress and the critic looked at each other and smiled. Then they both at once asked me to explain.

It was all so very simple. For six years a framed photograph of Jack Dempsey who had been a schoolboy hero of mine had hung in my little kitchen so that I could see it as I eat my meals. But Hitler had taken away the whole wall of that kitchen and the photo now lay in the rubble and was beyond repair. And the Egg? Oh I just fancied a nice egg, that's all. Mr Woollcott said that immediately he reached New York he would personally see about replacing the photo of Jack Dempsey, who he seemed to know quite well. (He did and all) but he said that he was no conjurer and could not conjure up a new laid egg.

¶ *Much ado about so very little.* *1949*

I was in Cotrone, a small port in the Gulf of Tarranto, a day's journey from Bari. I was the first Englishman they had seen for twelve years, the war passed them by. The Americans stationed at Bari never made the journey to this tiny and uninteresting place, its only feature being a

16th century Spanish fort, now the home of dozens of poor Italians, and a shack-town of hovels with a stench that fairly knocks you back.

Now, I was seated in a cafe in the small square which is the centre of the port, when a man came in and, looking at me, said aloud, 'ENGLISH . . . they stink', and spat on the floor. I could do nothing because he was with his pals and they could have so easily cut my throat and tipped me into the gulf of Tarranto and not a soul would have cared. It was wiser to be silent and alive. But when I left that cafe a man followed me and catching up with me apologised for the ill manners of his fellow countryman. He seemed a nice bloke and as the other passengers on the little cargo boat I had travelled on preferred the safety and the sanitary arrangements of our ship to Cotrone, I was alone and glad of someone to talk to.

This bloke spoke English very well. He told me some things about this part and the hope that it would soon become a very busy port for it had a marvellous natural harbour. He said that I really ought to see the sites and ruins of the Religious Order founded by Pythagoras. I hadn't the vaguest idea what on earth the bloke was talking about; but I enquired how one got to these ruins. It was easy. One got a rowing boat and a man to row one there to the extreme end of the gulf, and then there was a little walk. It would be a pleasant mornings' row and five shillings would cover and entirely please the boatman and that any man with a boat in the shanty town would take me. Indeed, if I wished for company this kind man would be so very proud and happy to be my guide. He would accept another 5s in English money please, for his services.

Indeed, if I care to give him ten shillings, he would see about the whole excursion for me and the boat would be by the side of the ship next morning at, say ten o'clock. Would that do? It would do, but I would *not* pay until the journey was completed and we were back against the side of my ship. Oh yes, I trusted him, it was *not* that, only one just had to be carefull – one hears such things you know. He saw that I was firm in the matter and we left it at that.

I don't think I expected to see the man the next morning. But there he was, and the boat and rower too.

The next morning was very pleasant with a cloudless sky and the atmosphere fresh. The sea looked calm. Oh well, in for a penny, in for ten shillings; so into the boat I got.

The old man rowed steadily for well over an hour with firm and steady strokes keeping close to the land. It was all so very peaceful. I could easily have gone to sleep but didn't for it was all quite new and unexplored territory to me. What did strike me was the strange and lifeless colour of the land, a strange greyish dull unhealthy colour, like as if all the land had been used for centuries and centuries without any fertilisers and was *dead*. Here and there one could see wretched trees and stems stern twisted and warped as if with the pain of years. These I was told were Olive Trees ... I had to accept the statement for I'd never seen like trees before. But if Olive is as weary as her trees, then she'd be no bed mate for Freddie nohow.

Miles we went, on and on, and then the coast line got a little rugged and jutted out like a small pensinula and there was a little bay. In the distance was a few weary looking trees and some hill-lets. My guide said that we were there and told the boatman to pull for the shore. When we got there he got close in and then pulled the boat up to land with us two still in his boat and out we got. I gave the rower a cigarette and he put it into his pocket without a word of thanks. Then I gave him a bread roll that I'd scrounged from the breakfast table. He tore this into half and eat both halves in two mouthfulls. He said *Grati* or thanks or something but he certainly seemed very pleased and wanted more. But I do not go around even in hungry towns like Cotrone with rolls in all my pockets. We left the man with his boat and I followed the guide.

Now, although from the boat it had all seemed very flat, the ground was very uneven with giant cracks in it and huge lumps of dull earth and then patches of dust: earth so fine that ones feet sunk into it and the slightest movement brought up clouds of dust – nasty dust like fine ashes that smarted and stung ones eyes – I had to follow my guide and for the most part of the journey I was behind him. He seemed so keen to get to this marvelous ruin. On and on we went. I was absolutely covered with dust and it was not a bit pleasant. Then it got a bit stoney and many times I nearly twisted my ankle. Then there were bits of rock and ten minutes more uncomfortable walking found us at *the site*, the very ancient site seen by few men.

Picture five or six weary old twisted trees growing in almost lifeless looking earth. Then four very large rocks. Each of them about twelve foot long and five foot wide all round – square pillers. One stands up at an angle like the brother to the tower of Pisa. Another four feet away lays down at the end of it another is resting so that you think that at a push of your foot it was topple over and lay beside its brother. The last of the huge pillars (if you think twelve foot long *is* huge) was some yards away and lay half buried in the earth. Thats all there was. There were no carvings or designs at all on any of the four rocks. 'Lo! We are *here!* Site of Mighty things Site of Pythagoras! Is it not wonderfull?' I knew the word to say and I *said it* loud and very clear! The rocks were unquestionably ancient. The centuries had worn them smooth. But just four rocks! No ruins, nothing whatsoever picturesque! They hadn't even the charm or mystery of Stonehenge.

I was never so disappointed. Miles and miles we had journeyed and there was I battered and hot and covered with dust and there was the foolish guide still carrying on about the site of learning. Very, very Ancient, seen by few English ... Pythagoras ... Great Wisdom. I said several rude words and then Home James and spare the blooming dust. And back we went over the uneven earth and the sun poured down and I got hotter and hotter.

By the time we got back to the boat I felt half dead. I was just getting into the boat when I saw in the distance a young woman bathing. She had on a one piece, just a pair of knickers with a couple of hankies tied over her breasts. She was dark and very pretty. I would say that she was around twenty-two and the bloom of youth was still upon her. She took no notice of us men, but we all noticed her. I said that I was going to have a little swim and they could wait for me. They were agreeable. Time meant nothing to them. I handed over a packet of cigarettes and stripped all save me little panties. I knew very well that I was taking a great risk. These men could have stolen my clothes and bit of cash, got into the boat and gone off, leaving me stranded with many, many miles to walk home. But Cotrone is a small place and the police there have a very firm hand on the residents, it would not really have been much worth their while.

I am not much of a swimmer but I do love a nice paddle, so I paddled over to the young lady, who was also doing more paddling than swimming. I said, 'Good afternoon. Lovely day'. And she replied in excellent English. I told her that I was a visitor from London on an Ellerman Cargo ship, merely a passenger. She said that she knew London very well and that one of her brothers sold ice cream near Hyde Park Gates. We chatted in a very pleasant manner. I told her all about the marvelous ruins and she said it was a Racket and that others had been sold the same tale. I asked where she got the word Racket from. She said that Bari had been the headquarters of the American forces during the war. She knew all the words. What was she doing in such a lonely spot? Getting away from people. But this is miles from anywhere. 'I know that,' she said. 'That's why I am here. Have a little hut,' and she pointed to over a ridge. 'Would you care to see it?' Her eyes were very inviting and so was her charming figure.

I was just going to say Yes – Yes to anything that she suggested, when I saw that on her neck about two inches from her ear was a large and ugly looking boil. Somehow that took all the romance out of the whole situation. Lonely beach, two men two hundred yards away, who were in my pay, young and well made woman, with her own hut, and the invitation in her eyes . . . *and a boil*. I said, 'No, thanks ever so much. I really must be getting back'. And wishing her a pleasant goodbye, I returned to the men.

My guide passed the remark that the woman looked pleasing. Perhaps I'd been too tired? She is very good—give you a nice time—speaks English ... and knows the ways of English, nice American ways. I didn't say a word. The man knew all about her. I am very sure that had it not been for a very common boil, I'd have visited a very common woman. The Gods protect the innocent. And yet it could not possibly have been a set-up. There are not enough visitors to this port. If they saw ten new faces in a year it would be a miracle. It was all so strange. I didn't care to solve the mystery. I got dressed and the row back to the ship was the one nice part of the venture.

I paid the men the ten shillings and just as we parted my guide said: 'I have another amazing site to show you, other side of Gulf—very ancient. Ten shillings, only that, nice ride ... nice girl as well. ten shillings for her. She come with us, we leave you, we return. after. *Yes?*' And I said, 'No!!' and I meant *no*. I didn't want to see any more ruins—in rocks or females.

* * *

¶ *Extract from a five minute talk I gave to a small Writers Club on the South Coast. 1949*

I am very sorry that there are a lot of I's in this little talk, but you see, I don't know what you do or how you do it. I only know what I do and the way I do it. You must not think that I have a great sense of my own importance, for if you do you wrong me. I most certainly have complete confidence and you will agree I am sure, that without confidence these days you can get nowhere ever so fast. When I have chewed the cud over in my mind as to exactly what I am going to write about, I set to work. And How – I just talk the whole thing out aloud to myself or to my very kind landlady, and when I have talked it out aloud, I then slowly put it down exactly as I have spoken it. I write as I talk and I talk as I write. A friend of mine named Willy Maugham told me to do this and I was wise enough on that occasion to accept the advice, because there is a man who knows his onions and also knows How Many beans make five. The advice was endorsed by Arnold Bennett. 'Talk it, then write it and if you say "ain't" and if you say "lor luv a duck" then put it down jest where you say it in ordinary conversation. That's to be your Style. . . . Your Literary Style.' And so for over twenty years its been my style and I've written over 2000 published articles and half a dozen books. You may have read my writings in *The Writer*. Well, there you have pretty good examples of my weird and wonderful literature, and as you read it I feel pretty sure that you not only are convinced that I know what I am writing about but that its sincere. I am really endeavouring to help the beginner to some measure of success.

¶ *A Romance in Three Stages. February 1950*

My 'steady' has gone from me. She has gone to hospital to be cured of her blackouts and the sickness of her poor mind which is the result of raid injuries. She is to go through much that I myself went through in 1942. It will take all of six months. Her last words to me as we parted today were: 'You are my steady, Freddy. I shall return to you'. And I have promised to wait for her. I shall wait one year if needs be. She is Scotch, fat and amiable, and so clean and tidy. She is a good honest girl and worth waiting for. I put my steady in the hands of God. Please make her well. Bring to her complete recovery. I shall write to her once or twice every week and keep faith with her.

¶ March 1950

My steady has been away a month and a half. She tells me she is having a drug treatment that keeps her in a daze and that she is unable to read or write and cannot cope with letters. Will I be patient and wait? o.k. steady, in silence I will wait, and I will pray for you every night, my dear. Get well soon. I'll be still here in Walworth awaiting you. Lizzie as well wrote a letter of encouragement and bestest wishes.

¶ Xmas Eve 1950

This day brought a bitter blow – or is it a Beautiful Brushoff? I should be happy, for tomorrow is Xmas day. Today I had a lovely present all ready for my steady girl friend, who has been away from me for nine months. I was going down to Surrey to take it to her home. I was going to hand it over to her parents, who would no doubt be visiting my girl on Xmas day and take my gift with them. The sight of my gift would remind her of her promise and of the man in Walworth who still awaits her complete recovery in order to carry on our romance that was marred by sickness.

This morning I got a letter from my 'dear one'. It read: 'Dear Fred, I am now back home and am absolutely cured and well. I have found Jack again, who I was engaged to six years ago and broke it off with because I was unwell. Those six years are sweeped away and we have found ourselves and happiness again. I wish you a merry Xmas, Yours truly, A . . .'

That, Diary, was my Xmas letter. Never had she mentioned Jack, Joe or Jeffery to me. She said that she was absolutely unattached and there was no one but me. There was no boy friend except me and she was grateful for my love and loyalty. And so I have waited nine months and am now left holding a baby of wasted dreams and futile plans.

Ain't some women real bitches! Blimey, a bitch dog would have more faith and loyalty. When she was ill no one but me wanted her. Now she is fit and well and up pops Jack who'd obviously been missing for six years. Only this fool of a Bason had remained loyal and waited – waited in silence because she insisted on silence, hoping and praying for her welfare each and every day. And now a Beautiful Brushoff on Xmas eve. The only kind thing that can be said is that it is complete and was no lingering torment. Well, well, I live to learn. Another lesson is learnt, although what the heck the lesson is I cannot in this moment of mingled emotions put upon paper.

¶ *November 2nd 1950*

Old man G. B. Shaw is now dead, and as he was ninety-four he'd had a very good innings. Already they are saying he'll be buried in Westminster Abbey. I bet he would *hate* that. The last writer to have an Abbey burial was Kipling, who was buried in the Poets Corner in 1936. But *what* corner would they put Shaw in – Yes, *what* corner? I suppose I ought to be exact. Shaw passed away peacefully at one minute to five o'clock this morning, November 2nd. I will wear me black tie for a week.

¶ *1950. Two London street games*

A boy age about ten was seated on a wall that was about five foot high. He was going 'Buzz Buzz Bang'. On the pavement looking up at him were three little boys, much younger. I asked the boy on the wall what on earth they were playing at. He said, 'I am an *Atom Bomb*'. 'Okay,' I said, 'You are an atom bomb. What are these three boys?' 'Oh them,' he replied. 'Them is the victims. You see, mister, if I jumps down sudden like and touches one of them, he's dead – real dead. And the game goes on untill all three of them are dead, see, mister?' I saw, and passed on with a sigh.

★ ★ ★

He was seated astride some railings. He had a piece of stick in one hand and a shopping bag in the other. He was going, 'Gee Up, Gee Up', and moving backwards and forwards as if upon a horse. I asked him what the game was and he said that he was playing *Lester*. It was quite a new one on me and so I gave him a sweet and asked him to explain. Bless his heart, he did. He was Lester Piggott the famous boy jockey – so it was called *Lester* and not *Racehorses*. I could see why he needed the stick, to help drive the horse, but could see no reason for the bag. He explained that as well. He was riding in The Hunt Cup. And the bag? the bag was for the Hunt Cup when he had won it. He had it all worked out.

¶ *Thursday December 21st 1950*

Today just about noon I was passing the National Gallery when I saw a well dressed lady, coming towards me who I thought I recognised. I said to her, 'Excuse me, *I'm* Fred Bason, the Fred Bason of *Fred Bason's Diary*'. (I thought I'd give me book a plug even if I proved wrong.) 'Surely you are Joyce Carey?' And it was.

We seemed quite pleased to meet each other after about a two year break. She told me that she'd read my *Diary* and thoroughly enjoyed it (which shows her good taste) and expressed the hope I would write another. To which I said I'd do eight, if I did not run out of material. She asked why eight and I explained that James Agate had done nine *Egos* and I would go one beneath the master; although I had just as much ego as he had I was different in so much, so that I would never depend on other folk's letters to fill up my diaries with. I said I'd no wish to be a second Agate. She said, 'Quite right too. You be the first Fred Bason, it's so much better! I promise you I will read the whole eight of your diaries.' And at that, with 'Merry

Christmas' on both sides, we parted after a warm hand-shake.

Why put this in my Diary? Well, at least I know *one buyer* (with some influence) of Diary 3, if I get as far as that, and do not dry up of material I personally deem worth the printing! The other reason is that it's the second time I've worn my trilby, which Liz says makes me look distinguished and upholds my position to the world of literature. And I was able to *raise* my hat like a little gent to Joyce, whereas had it been another time I'd have just touched my cap. No sane man raises from his head his cap because that puts his hair all out of place for the back of the cap always catches the hair as it comes off and the hair sticks out like a cockatoo's comb – it's also so difficult to replace a cap without the aid of a mirrow at that right cheeky angle with which you started out. I tried to take me cap off when I saw a lady I know but gave it up after seeing myself reflected in a mirrow with me cap in me hand as I spoke to Greta Garbo (she *didn't* reply – but, what the hell, some people wouldn't even attempt to speak to this woman). I looked real untidy. After all, when I wore a cap I merely *touched* it at the people as a sign of respect but never, never removed it. Now I have a trilby I can do so without my bit of hair rucking up. Just two years ago I wouldn't have cared a heck about my appearance, but when you know 10,000 people and when ten million people know you are alive, you simply just have to be a bit nearer the mark. Oh no, diary, I ain't gorn all snobbish – it's just *plain common sense* – Lizzie's brand!

* * *

¶ *December 1950*

The integrity of a seller of books is a very precious thing. Always I have tried so very hard to supply my clients with exactly their especial requirements. I think that after thirty years in and around bookselling I reached the apex of my career when today I visited the offices of Ridley's Wine Circular in the City. Over a number of years I have supplied the editor of this trade journal with books about wine. Yesterday I purchased as a sheer gamble *The Wine Trade Directory for 1900*. It is 10 × 6 and is mostly addresses of wine firms, some wine data and many blank pages to put trade notes on. It seemed unique, so I paid the 5s asked and it was well packed up for me. Today, I did not reopen the parcel but immediately took it over (for 3d fares). At the office I asked for Hugh Stephen, the editor. He was out. So I said to a strange (but nice) lady, 'I have a book on the wine trade and its 7s 6d and I am Fred Bason'. And she said, 'As you are Fred Bason it is sure to be good – and right there and then from a drawer she gave me 7s 6d and she did *not open the parcel!* I thanked her and out I went. 3d more to get home. 2s profit! And as Hugh never sent it back and as Ridleys is still going strong, I suppose it was ok.

¶ *1950*

Cor luv a duck, I must have arrived somewhere. An artist named Bernard Hailstone is doing me in oils. Yes, I am having meself done as an oil painting. He is making no charge, and so I am making no charge either, although

I do think its a waste of both our times. I have allowed him two hours every Wednesday untill it's finished. That's all the time I can spare to this luxury. He has just told me by way of interest (I suppose) that he happens to be the fifth cousin of Georges Carpentier, the one time famous boxer. That staggered me. I said, 'With such blue and distingusied blood in your veins I should be doing *you* in oils if I could!' I do hope we don't have any Hailstones during the sittings, for the light in Walworth is at no times very good. Fancy having me face done in oils. Well, well, and yet another WELL.

¶ *December 1950*

I have never before ever recorded in my diary who sent me Xmas Cards. I think it's about time I did this (only wish I'd thought of it before). I've limited the list to the first 24 I got, for in all I had 247 and it would fill three pages to list 'em all (although Bless 'em all). These were the first 24. A.A. Milne, the author: Jack Cappell, a Boxing promotor: Mercy Ambrose, a maternity nurse, who is intelligent and sweet: R. C. Hutchinson, another noted author and a fan of mine: Ann Nelson, one of my very few Irish fans: Enid Hollins, an Australian one-time actress, who now writes splendid plays and needs just a bit of luck to make front page news: Hilda Figgis-Smith, who owns a thatched cottage in Devon: Grace Murphy, one of my ardent U.S.A. admirers, age 74: F. Cowlin, in Canada, who signs every letter 'EFF' and who for so long I thought was a man but is very much a lady: Mrs Wood-house, of Eastbourne, in whose house I have lodged on my week's holiday once a year there: Ruth Duchers, who is a lovely lady with a kind heart: Harold Peers, who runs the Book dept of Kendal Milne, the Manchester firm, one of my so few readers inside my own trade: Lt. Col. W. Lyon, of the *Horseman's Year Book* and who is a very noble English gentleman – one of the few men in the world I take me cap off too! Dorothy Clark of Surbition, who is very much a fan but who ticks me off like a mum when I get a little cocky: Alan Steele, a Bookman who has been a loyal reader of my writings since the start: Nick Bentley, the humourist, whose work I so much admire: John Foster White, publicity manager of Grayson and Grayson, who are *not* my publishers: Frank Sturrock, my insurance agent, and a wise man when I need sane and canny advice!: Frank Tilsley, one of my favourite authors and who puts a kind word in for me when ever he's able: Beatrice Winkler, my most precious American reader and one of my most precious pals: Betty Webb, a little girl who works amongst books, age sixteen. I wish she was twenty-six, she is a sweet child: Ruth Draper, the great American actress and a precious fan of mine: Frank Pettingell, the noted actor and a real pal of mine – we have so many likes in common, like collecting books and cigarette cards.

The first card of the season came from A. A. Milne and the last from Betty Webb and everyone of the 247 got a reply. Again a lonely Xmas. But I had my lovely cards for company and spent the whole time writing.

¶ *Things which occur to me (an undated page which I found in my Diary). 1950*

Isn't a sense of good clean fun valuable? From Bristol I had a fan mail letter from Stephanie, which ended 'your fan till peaches grow on elm trees'. From Greymouth, a place in New Zealand, I got a weird fan mail letter. I will put it down exactly as I got it, and it cost 1s 3d to send it and there was a couple of New Zealand stamps to value of 1s 3d to reply with.

'Dear Mr Bason, We have just read the latest edition of *The Saturday Book. Are you Real?* We are suspicious. If you are real and are reading this you will be amused. You expose your character so much in your writings that you cannot be anything else but amused, but we should very, very much like to know if you are real. Your sincere and faithfull fans, Rusell and Thelma.'

What on earth do I reply? It's cost them 2s 6d to ask this silly question. If I answer 'yes' how can I convince them? If I send them my photo how are they to know that me is me? Of course, I could go to New Zealand and let them stick a pin in me so that I call out OH! and they know then I am alive. I have discided to answer a silly letter with a silly reply.

'Dear Fans, No, I am not real. I am G. Bernard Shaw in disguise, come back to this earth with no beard, no brogue and very few H's this time, as a Cockney to have another Basonfull. But if Thelma ever cares to brave the wilds of Walworth, I am very willing, mood and time permitting, to prove how real I am.'

¶ *December 1950*

Entirely out of the blue and completely unexpected I have received a signed photograph from Annette Mills of Muffin and TV Fame. A very friendly letter thanking me for praising in my columns the latest Muffin book. Little does she remember that over twenty-two years ago she gave me a photo of herself at the stage door of the Coliseum when she was appearing on that stage as a 'good humoured dancer'. I've just put the photos side by side and allowing for the great art of the photographers of today I really must say that Annette has worn very very well indeed. Would she like to be reminded of twenty-two years ago? Is she *still* all that good humoured? Anyrate, I've been a very loyal fan. And there's another lady who I see I've been a fan of for the same twenty-two years. Her name is Richmal Crompton, of the *Just William* fame. I think that as a pleasant surprise I will send back to Richmal this Christmas the Christmas card which she sent to me twenty-two years ago. That ought to make a *very* pleasant surprise.

★ ★ ★

¶ *January 10th 1951*

I have been told that only *one* in every thirty Russians are Communists and party members, that's to say that one in thirty are died in the wool out and out *Reds*. It's perfectly obvious to me that Communism is an ideal, an idea and a religion. But *only* for *Reds*. Well now, say you go to war with the Russians (which God forbid) you will kill lots of Russians (and lots of English as well) but I am very sure that you can't kill an ideal or a religion and you have got nowhere at all because twenty-nine in thirty are not party members and are merely Russians, and I can't see why you have to try to kill a bloke just because he happens to be born a Russian! The real Bosses of the Reds, the real Communists, don't and would not fight at the front. You don't see the Attlees, Morrisons, King George, The Bishop of Gloster or anyone else like these people right bang at the front (not, of course, that they are Reds). They direct. It's the young that get killed! There must be classes. No one is really equal. I loathe titles, but I would never be a Communist NEVER. All this here means I don't think we shall fight Russia – ever!

¶ *1951*

A Mr Kamer, an American on business in Turkey saw my photograph and two columns about me and me writings in *Time* magazine. He made a note in his diary that should he ever reach London he'd see two things for sure. Sadlers Wells Ballet and ME. He was unable to get a seat at the ballet the night he wanted so he set out to find me instead. He asked just by the way in the actual *box office* of Covent Garden Opera House if they happened to know of me and where I could be located. Oh yes, indeed they knew of me and they told him what bus to get on (a 68 from Waterloo Bridge to my road). They said they did not know the number but I was so famous that anyone in the road would know. He arrived at the top of my road. He asked five residents in the road where I lived and not one of them had *heard* of me. He asked six others before he actually asked Lizzie. She brought him in. Result, three pleasant hours company.

¶ *February 19th 1951*

I read a case in the paper today that disgusted me! A man walking along a country lane sees a pile of shingle. Remembering his fowls badly needed something to pick at, the man puts some shingle in his pocket – two pence worth, about a quarter of a pound, and as he was doing so a copper turned up (as they so seldom do when they *are* wanted) and told him he was stealing, so the man emptied his pocket. But the copper would have none of that – and, later, the man was fined £1 in a court. ok. He did something wrong – poor citizen. He gets a black mark on his character. The copper probably gets a nice red mark on his promotion card and if he gets twelve more, they'll make him a sergeant! I wonder what the shingle man thinks of the copper?

Sometimes British Justice is queer. You really can't wonder that the average citizen hates the police and avoids the law in every way possible. Even a very important lawyers told me two months ago that the law is an ass and only millionaires or fools go to law. And he makes his living from Law! What of us poor citizens, when there are 25,000 by-laws and regulations that can put us foul of the law and make criminals of us? Us All? Not quite all. The rich and the 'wide boys' *seem* to get round the regulations. I know a pretty famous author. Ask him to give a lecture. Sure – it will be 150 guineas at the least. But what is a mere £152 10s od to him? – over half would go in income tax. He gets a choice box of cigars and a case of wiskey. He gets some sheep for his farm – oh, he gets 'graft' and to hell with his eightpence worth of meat. And

D

the wide boys? They get nylons. West-end actresses don't quibble over price 'when it comes to the real nylons and no questions asked'—and it's cash, and no one is the wiser. And so it goes on. I wish I knew where they get nylons for nixes to sell at a fiver!

But I don't know. Sometimes right deep in my heart I wonder *if* honesty really *is* the *best* policy! I see the wide boys around The Elephant and Castle. They pay £20 for their suits—*cash!* My suit is seven years old and cost £3. They put £5 on the nose of a horse and if it loses they shrug their padded shoulders. I put 2s on a dog occasionally and me and Lizzie worry all night till the papers arrive next morning and we then know the result of our investment. It's true that we usually win—and if I was less of a gambler in books and more of a gambler on the dogs I could win a great deal of money. But I won what I intended to win—banked it and never gamble.

You want to know my system, brother? Sure, I'll tell you. There is no secret about it *now* because I gave it to readers of *The Saturday Book* way back in 1948. You simply and solely bet on substituted dogs. You compare the *forecasted* runners in a Friday paper with the actual runners in a Saturday paper. You will often find that overnight a dog has been substituted for another for some reason or other. You bet on that substitute—that reserve dog. For preference you bet it for a *place only* on the tote with a mild bet to win with a bookmaker. On average there are four substitutes each Saturday (and often more) over all the London race tracks and its very seldom that less than two don't win! Times again all four get a place. Sometimes all four win! When they all come up trumps me and

Liz take Monday off and go to the pictures and have 1s 9d seats instead of 1s 3d. That's how we got the money to see James Stewart in *Harvey* on February 19th 1951 – see! But we bet only 2/- where once I betted £20. There comes a time when one must stop – when luck gives out. I know when to stop.

¶ *March 1951*

The last six months or so have been cruel to the Theatre. Shaw, Bridie, C. B. Cochran, and now, today, Ivor Novello dead. Ivor died just as he would have liked to have died – well, nearly, for perhaps he'd have liked to have died *on* the Palace stage surrounded by flowers and wenches. He missed that exit by only four hours, so he was nearly in harness. I have only two recollections of him. Near twenty-six years ago I took a girl I was very fond of to the Brixton Theatre to see him in, I think, *The Rat*. We sat in The Gods. She was so smitten with him. She said that I could never make love to her the way dear Ivor made love and I *lost her*. Yes, I lost her, for she constantly compared me with Novello. 'Ivor would *never* do *that* . . . or say *that* . . . like *that*.' I got real fed up with the comparison. We had a row. She said it was all *my* fault. If I'd never taken her to see Ivor she'd have been *satisfied* with *me*. And from that first seeing she became a fan of his for life.

I met her about five years ago (still single). We chatted, pleasantly, and she confessed that she had seen *Glamourous Nights* thirty-seven times, *Careless Rapture* thirty-five times and *Dancing Years* thirty-nine occasions, paying every time. I told Novello of this profitable fan I made for him and he said that he felt that he ought to compensate me. But I described his fan and we then agreed that she hadn't worn well and I had perhaps had a good miss.

Novello gave lots of pleasure to millions. Ought to have been knighted. Twenty years ago he wrote about Galleryites for my book *Gallery Unreserved*. The book being quite unobtainable now I think I ought to put in my diary his MS in case I lose the original. Here is what Novello wrote exclusively for me in 1931.

'So much has been written for and against the boys and girls who are styled Galleryites that I think we may have lost, slightly, our sense of proportion. My personal experience of galleryites is largely coloured by an affection for them. For, after all, my first enthusiastic tribute came from the upper regions and while the stalls saw fit to reserve judgement, the gallery was always full to capacity.

I think that far too much is written about the so-called temperament of the gallery. To me the gallery is to all intents and purposes the ordinary playgoer, slightly tempered by more pronounced enthusiasms either for or against. In all my experience of the stage, the only rough gallery that I have experienced was on the first night of *Sirocco* and as I left the stage door (by the way, never has there been a larger crowd outside a stage door after any of my first nights) I heard two voices say, "We expected better".

A very strong point about the galleryites is that they are not in the least prejudiced, and the fact that they have taken strong exception to one play does *not* mean that they will not be delighted with the next, even if played by the same actors and written by the same author. So many actors have said to me: "I cannot think why they don't close the gallery on first nights: hysteria is no good to the actors or the play". Oh, how entirely I disagree with them, for the first night would lose all its electric atmosphere were such an unthinkable thing to happen as the closing of the gallery. No audience could be more rapt and silent than the boys and girls up there and, if they decide that it is thumbs down to a production, they have just as much right to show their disapproval as have the stalls and dress circle to damn with faint praise. One thing is certain. People who wait eight to ten hours outside a theatre for appallingly uncomfortable seats are prepared to enjoy the performance. I wish as much could be said for the regular list of first-nighters, a considerable number of whom are *sure* that the evening is going to be one long calamity.'

(signed) Ivor Novello

This article took him twenty minutes to think and type and that was on our first meeting when I was to him an absolute stranger and asked if he would care to write a few words for a theatre book, and I was sorry that I could not pay him for it. He was so kind. His fans will miss him: reckon they will keep his name ever-green, like that of Valentino is still kept green, although Rudolph is now a bit mouldy. I had tea with one of the chorus boys in a Novello show in 1950 and he said Ivor is very loyal to his many friends and always tries to find a part for them in his shows. His fans are loyal as well. They will always remember Ivor.

¶ *April 6th 1951*

This day I was kindly invited to a little party in the home of Clifford Bax in Albany, Piccadilly. The company consisted of Sir Arnold Bax, Harriet Cohen, Kathleen Hewitt (handsomest woman writer I've seen in years), Clifford Bax, G. B. Stern (a real old friend of mine; hadn't seen her for ten years), and last but by no means least the kind lady who'd invited and took me there, Meum Stewart (she is a fan of mine and that's why, I suppose, I was invited to this little do? For it couldn't have been for my music, as I did not attempt to play the lovely piano after Sir Arnold and Harriet had obliged us. Well, even I know me place). I could see after a little while that the conversation was a trifle guarded, as if they thought what they said might be used as evidence *against* them. So I ups and I says, 'Although I am getting a bit known for my diaries, there *are* times when I keep my trap shut and forget what is said. This is one of those days!' After that it was such a pleasant hour – and I will say no more!

¶ *Two short letters and two short answers. February 5th 1951*

From S.W.3.
'Dearest Freddie Bason. I have thoroughly enjoyed your work not only in *The Saturday Book* (better than ever) but in your diary which I consider delightful. Would you do me the honour of coming to tea on Sunday to see my signatures? *Please!*

—— (Miss)

¶ *From 152 Westmoreland Road, S.E.17*

Dear Miss. In the good old days the villain used to say 'Come up and see my etchings'. In these modern times the miss now says, 'Will you come up and see my signatures! But, Heck, Lady, I've nothing to lose! Yes, I *will* be there at four to see your signatures and I hope they are well rounded!

— Fred Bason (Mr)

¶ *From S.W. 3*

Dear Mr Bason. Allow me the privilege of changing my mind. My signatures are, alas, not rounded at all and would bore you to tears.

Yours, etc. —— (Mrs)

¶ *From 152 Westmoreland Road, S.E.17*

Dear Mrs —— Thank you for sparing my tears. I do hope your husband enjoys looking at your signatures for years and years and all keeps fine and dandy. Good luck.

Yours, etc. Fred Bason (still *Mister*)

★ ★ ★

¶ *April 6th 1951*

I was standing in Trafalgar Square waiting for a bus to take me to High Wycombe in order to deliver a lecture in the Public Library when a very old man came up to me. The time was 4.45. He looked a nice clean old man and he had a very fine Father Christmas beard. He was dressed in a suit of old oddments and there was a banjo slung over his shoulders. He touched the peak of a very battered trilby and then said, 'Can I get me to Bond Street from here in ten minutes? It's *very* important. Must be there at five to five'.

I said that it was easy to get either end or in the middle of Bond Street well within ten minutes, by getting on a bus to Piccadilly Circus and then walking past the Royal Academy – or a bus, number 12, would go up Regent Street and by getting off halfway down and popping through any street on the left, one could be in Bond Street inside six minutes, or, by keeping on that bus and going round by Oxford Circus, you'd come to the top end of Bond Street in around eight minutes. He said that half way down was where he wanted to be and he waited beside me for a No. 12 bus.

I wondered why the poor old man wanted to be in Bond Street by five to five, he looked so out of place. I wanted to know the answer. Yes, I know, diary, I was being sheer 'nosey'. I asked outright with no beating around the bush. 'Old gent,' I said, 'Why *must* you be there at five to five? It's worth sixpence to you if I gets an interesting reply.' He replied, 'You are civil. I will not take your sixpence – not unless you thinks it worth it. It's like this here. I am seventy-nine. I am told that in Bond Street there's a block of offices above a fashion shop. In that block is a lot of young ladies. They come out of that place at a few minutes after five. When they hear me playing Old Jim – that's me banjo – and when they see my beard they will give money to me. I will earn, they tell me, anything around two shillings in ten minutes. But I have to be there just before they all come out for, if they see me starting up my music, they will know that I've only just arived and consider me a fraud, having not earnt the money. But if I am really *at* my music when they come out, they will not know how long I have been there. Besides that, young ladies like to get home to their sweethearts quickly and do not linger at work when work time is over, and likely within six minutes the whole of the offices will be cleared of the staff. These things have to be studied by the busker. Two minutes can mean all the difference when one is a public entertainer. Get to a theatre queue as the audience is actually going in and you may earn sixpence. Get there and play just one selection with an eye on the doors opening and get the hat round just two minutes before the doors open and you can get 2s for your work. I trust that I have satisfied your curiosity adequitly.'

'Yes, mate,' I said, and I handed him the tanner.

My bus arrived and I saw that his was in the distance. We parted, he to his pitch and me to my lecture. He'd have music. I only have my unmusical voice – and *no* Beard to charm my audience with. I was paid 42s for my hour's work. I shall never know what Father Christmas earnt in Bond Street.

★　★　★

¶ *June 1951*

Not much usually happens in June because it's my holiday month and one week I goes to Eastbourne or Bournemouth in me oldish clothes, looking like nothing on earth. I forgets all about books or writing and has me a nice restfull holiday. But this year I accepted an invite out of sheer curiosity and so went to the first Garden party of my life – at Eastbourne.

I was introduced as Frederick Bason, the famous Cockney author and lecturer. Then I said 'How do you do?' (which I shortened to How do?) thirty-seven times to thirty-seven strangers who I never expect to see again, and truly can't say that I care a dam how they do or not. I got very very dry and me stiff coller was chocking me, so I escaped any more How people did and had two cups of tea that was lukewarm and very wishy washy as I sat on a hard seat neath a nice big tree. There was a lot of nasty flies and mosquities around me, and when a lady brought a jam tart across to me, there was a nasty wasp on it which put the wind up me. So I looked at my watch, got up quickly, made me way to the exit and called a cab, which took me back to me lodgings where, after a rest on the bed minus coller and tie, I cooled off, put on me old clothes again and became Fred Bason, seller of cheap books who does a bit of writing now and again, when he's not broadcasting on radio or platform.

No more garden parties. Alright for them that likes flies, wasps and mosquities and things what hang down from trees and dangle at your flipping earhole, but me, I prefer the party out of the garden and the company to be *under* forty years old and not so blooming catty about what the other person is wearing. This was a snooty affair.

¶ *He doesn't live there any more. August 1951*

It was Sunday afternoon and having finished my fan mail and posted it I was at a lose end and a trifle browned off, so I took myself for a walk down Blackfriars Road. At the corner where The Ring (famous Boxing Hall) used to be, I paused to recapture scenes of my youthfull days when I would be inside or outside The Ring on a Sunday afternoon capturing the autographs during the Boxing show. Then I noticed some imposing houses in the distance and found myself in Nelson Square for the first time in my life, and was interested to see a plaque upon one of the houses to the effect that Percy Shelley lived in the house in the long distant past. It was a very nice looking house and seemed to have escaped the blitz – at least, the structure seemed intact but the bottom windows were boarded up with corrugated iron. The house was empty and I naturally wondered why. I should have loved to live in a house where Shelley once worked and lived.

On my return home after my jaunt I said to Lizzie, 'I had a nice little walk and I saw the House in Nelson Square where Percy Shelley used to live!' 'Used to live?' says she. 'Yes, he's gone now and the house is empty,' says me. 'Oh,' says Liz, 'perhaps he's moved into the L.C.C. Flats.'

I can now very well understand why the authorities of Southwark don't pay too much attention to the literary relics of the district. Liz has never heard of Shelley in her whole life. We toasted the memory of Shelley that evening in glasses of Sherry which a dear kind fan W. James sent to us last Christmas.

¶ *August 13th 1951*

Tonight I was at Caxton Hall for the monthly meeting of the London Writers Club. They have a lot of would-be authors but don't seem to have many who are actually living by their pen. As I was extra early, I was asked if I would be doorman and collect the one shilling from the visitors. Well, someone has to do it, and I'd not done it for many a month. I had collected 4s when a very attractive American visitor arrived. I asked her to sign the visitors book and then I took her one shilling. At seven I closed the door and handed over five shillings from the visitors. Then I saw that no one had chummed up or even spoken to the American visitor, so I went up to her and suggested that it would be more pleasant for her to sit in the second row with me than in the tenth row by herself. She agreed with such a nice smile and we soon made ourselves acquainted.

I do detest Cliques in clubs. In the interval I give the lady my card and glancing at it she says 'Goodness me, I have been longing to meet you. You are one of the *musts* of my visit to London. Read your diary way out in New York. Want to write a profile of you for American magazines. Only this day I enquired your address'. From then onwards we got along like a house afire and moved to the back of the hall and in low tone had a lovely talk and took not a bit of notice of the lecture. Rude of us, of course, but I am so sure we lost so little as the speaker was telling how to write fiction for woman's magazines . . . and I never write fiction and neither does the u.s.a. lady.

She asks me lots of questions and puts all the answers in a notebook. After the lecture was over we went for tea and cakes in a café in Victoria Street and chatted for another hour. She was a very pretty girl and said that at one time she was assistant editor to *The New Yorker* – or was it *Esquire?* Any rate, it was a top notch U.S.A. mag and she certainly seemed to know all her onions. I invited her to have tea at my home on Thursday.

¶ *August 16th. Thursday*

The Lovely American journalist has been and gone. We had *eels* for tea, as a great treat to me from Liz. And then we had a tin of oranges. The lady seemed to enjoy this rather weird English tea. She this time says she is Audrey Davenport and been on staff of *Esquire* and *Coronet*. She left 152 at six o'clock: at six twenty both me and Liz were *sick*. Eels and Oranges don't mix. I hope that Audrey got home alright.

¶ *August 1951*

I really must put on record that this month was the first time I had ever drunk champange. Yus, I know I ought to have done so before I was 40, but some how I'd always missed it (sherry is my favourite drink). Strangely enough I had it twice in the same night in different houses.

I was a long weekend guest in a house in the Midlands and on the last night my host brought out a highly expensive looking bottle of champange to celebrate something or other – maybe my *going* away? Any rate I was given two glasses and it went down like a treat and made me merry. A little later my host and I went with another guest to a nearby house for a coming-home party, and lo and behold I hadn't been in the house five minutes when I was again given champange, an even larger glass full. I drunk it down and then a bloke comes up to me and says he's D—, Lord D—, so with three glasses of champange inside me I looks sadly at him and I says, 'Well, you can't help that...can you...cock?' And he seemed to pass out as I passed by. I knew that him and me would not have a thing in common to talk about, and anyway I loathe titles.

I had four glasses of champange in that house and then I was well away. I did not care even if it snowed, although that would have been a miracle on that lovely August night. I sat at the piano and played some tunes and then my own host, who'd took me to this high class do, together with my fellow guest, volunteered to sing a song. They were going to sing *I may be wrong but I think you're wonderful*—with the drinks inside of them it would have been really wonderfull if either knew any of the words—and the wonderfull thing didn't happen. Neither of them knew anything but the first line and the song went rather like 'I may be wrong *but...but* I think you are wonderfull, I may be wrong *but...but* I er...er...think you are wonderfull', and then the needle stuck...and there they stood like a couple of twirps. And so I played *Three blind mice*, for that's what we were. Then suddenly the lights went out. I suppose that it was a fuse or one of the wives putting an end to our miserable exhibition. Anyrate, they sidled out of the room by the light of a candle and I slided off the piano stool and followed 'em, and we all went back home. And back home we 3 laughed ourselves to tears. We'd had a lovely time at that party. No one else had.

¶ *September 1951*

In a typewriter company in Blackfriars Road I found a very pretty girl. I sent to her one of my books nicely signed and with a kind letter hoping that we could be friends and could I take her out sometimes. After a long silence I got her reply: 'I enjoyed your book but I must be frank with you. I much prefer the company of animals to men'. I did not write to her again. Well!

¶ *October 20th, 1951*

Not a word ever from Audrey Davenport. Did we kill her or shock her with eels and oranges? She promised to write from Vienna. She is probally in Timbuctoo by now. I wish her well wherever she may be. The prettiest woman writer I have ever seen. Good luck to her. Far too good for the likes of me but it was nice to dream. Oh how they come and go in my life.

¶ *December 1951*

Nobody knows everything. To learn is often pleasant, so I put in my diary bits from an interesting letter from a Mr Bacon who wrote this week from Swansea. Now I did not know this Mr Bacon, for the only one I'd heard of was Francis, and he's a bit dead. This one is no ancester of same but tells me that he is a connection with the Bacon of Perkins, Bacon and Petch. I said to myself, so what? They sounded either like lawyers or brewers, or even a music hall act. Then I found out via letter that this here

Perkins and Bacon and Petch were the printers of the original postage stamp, i.e. the Penny Black.

Well, on the grounds that I have an interest in most things hobbyist, I was interested to learn that the picture on that stamp came from a medal which was made by William Wyon. It was first struck when Queen Victoria visited the City of London in 1837 – and so pleased everyone that it was used for the first stamp as well. Mr Bacon says that the first sheets of Penny Blacks were printed in twelve rows across and twenty rows down, making two hundred and forty stamps to a sheet; and if I come upon a stray sheet in my travels I can sell it to him and on the proceeds I can go to America and even afford to take Betty Grable out to dine. He also says that it was possible to wash off the cancellation mark from stamps of the penny black period and use them all over again (which is proper handy for folks like me with large fan mail). Fred Heath engraved the die for the Penny Black and same Fred Heath did some Christmas card and other designing in later years. These stamps were not perforated and had to be cut with scissors. I can see some of the most uncivil post office civil servants doing same today. 'Two hundred and forty stamps, please – here's a quid. Please cut them into seperate stamps, as I have a lotta mail to answer.'

The Penny Black was changed to penny Red in the year 1841, but was not as popular as the Black had been but the officials could see if they had been washed and used again. I think this is all very interesting. I most certainly did not know anything of this. I thought that Rowland Hill was the pioneer, assisted by Henry Cole (who is another of Christmas card fame, for I think the Cole cards were the very first illustrated uniform genuine British Christmas cards to appear in England, and I said so in Television in 1950 and no one wrote to say that I was wrong). The Penny Blacks were on sale in 1840.

Mr Bacon did not tell me if Perkins, Bacon and Petch are still printers, but states that he himself does a bit of printing, which can mean anything. What strikes me so strange out of this information is that of all these names, Perkins, Bacon, Petch, Cole, Wyon Heath, only one name seems to be known to anyone at all. Rowland Hill gets all the credit – and poor old Bacon ain't known at all. But that's the same with Francis Bacon. Old Bill Shakespeare gets nearly all the credit.

★ ★ ★

¶ *1951*

She is at least sixty-five and a Miss. I don't doubt for a moment that she hasn't a penny in the world except her old age pension – but she spends at least five shillings a week of it feeding creatures of God (as she calls them) in the shape of mangy dirty unwanted and smelly cats. Summer or winter, rain or shine, there she goes every day to a bomb site behind the Camberwell Green and there wait for her daily at least fifteen cats.

In the large shopping bag which she carries always there are the tops of coffee tins and these are the saucers and trays for the cats food. She places those tins on the floor and then brings out of newspaper fish bits that she has purchased and cooked. Into each tray goes the same amount, there are no favourites. But the stranger is welcome and I have seen that 15 go as high as 23 – but

never higher – and to each there was a little fish meal and
an interchange of views of this that and the other, for the
old lady talks to each of the cats as they are feeding and
they look up at her – like as if they *do* know what she is
saying to them.

I catch a glimpse of the party each time I go to the
pictures at The Odeon at Camberwell Green, for I make
it a point of going to this cinema early in the afternoon
so as to allow my seat to be vacant for someone who is at
work all the day and cannot get there untill the evening.
Its usually around 1.15 that the party for the strange cats
commences. I have never been present when the meal was
over and she collects the tins.

Only once have I spoken to this very kind old lady. I
asked her why on earth she did it, when they looked such
a nasty lot of cats. She answered with a quiet and simple
dignity, 'They are all creatures of God – like you and like
me. There homes were all around here and they got
bombed out. Thoughtless people moved away and forgot
their cats, and these simple creatures could not find other
homes. Someone has to feed them and it gives me great
pleasure to be allowed to do so'. I offered her five bob to
carry on the great work with. She refused it. She said that
one must pay for ones pleasures and this was her one
pleasure in life. I wonder what will happen, how the cats
will feel the day this kind old lady is taken away from
her pleasure and from this world of ours. Will some one
else take her place? I hope so.

¶ *What a Dodge. 1951*

A wide boy has kindly told me how he makes a £1 a
week so easily. Cor, what a way to make an easy quid!
Its a twist in a way – but only in a minor way – but then
the wide boy said he apologises if he gets found out. *Now
learn it!* You *palm* a ha'penny. Next you get a pencil – yes,
any sort or shape of pencil. Now you are in a sort of
gathering and you say to anyone, 'Lend me a shilling and
I'll show you an astounding trick'. The 1s is loaned to you.
Ok? Now you put the 1s on top of the pencil and hold it
there (ha'penny still in your palm) and you say to the
party, 'Is the 1s on the wood or on the lead of the pencil?'
Now it doesn't matter *what* he answers – as soon as he's
answered you say, 'Oh, why didn't you tell me that you
know the trick', and with a smile you put the pencil in
your pocket and as you put the pencil away you put the
1s in the same pocket, and give him the ha'penny, you've
had palmed! And in eight cases out of twelve, the man
will accept the coin and *without looking at it*, put it back
into his pocket. Why look at it? He saw the 1s on top
of the pencil and never thought you gave him a ha'penny,
and so he's 11½d short and you make at least £1 a week.
Cor!

¶ *1951*

I really must put it down. It happened ten years ago.
I'd been rather badly injured in the blitz and was for a
while in hospital near Watford. Whilest there I learnt that
Emlyn Williams play at The Globe Theatre was shortly

to end and I do so very, very much want to see it and Angela Baddeley who is so very sweet and talanted. I was very lame in both legs. Impudently I wrote to him asking if he could pull a string or two which would enable me and a nurse to come and see his play from a seat in the pit at the end of a row so that I could be carried in and put in the end seat and then not move till the show was over.

I did not know him, he did not know me. I had never written to him before in all my life, but Bless his generous heart, he sent me two stall seats for nurse and me at the end of the second row. The commander at the Red Cross Hospital was a solid and manly woman and you'd think she was harder than even iron, but she had a kind heart. A car was going to London. All was laid on. A nurse came with me. The gent with the car carried me in, and the nurse held me hand all the whole play and although it was a sad play we both had a lovely time. I sent a letter of thanks to Emlyn Williams and he replied that the pleasure was his. We have never met. His autograph was on the letters containing the tickets and the nice letter of 'not at all . . . a pleasure'. I feel that I ought to put on record this great kindness to an utter stranger.

¶ *Some of my treasures. Written in 1951 – last day of the year and finished 1st day of 1952*

In the days before world war two it was possible on certain nights of the week to go from Liverpool Street station to Southend by any train after six o'clock at night, for an evening by the sea (that's if the blooming tide wasn't out so that you could see the sea at Southend) at a specially reduced rate. Me and Liz (that's me landlady, in case you don't know by now) used to avail ourselves to this smell of the winkle-barges and whelk stalls very often, for one could be on the sea front by around seven o'clock and stay untill about ten. It was very good value and such a change from Walworth.

Well, one evening we got down there and was walking down the High Street somewhat slowly, looking in all the shops, for it was raining. Lizzie paused to look at some frocks next door to a cinema and as I waited I looked at the film star photos displayed in a panel in front of the cinema. Now, there was a man by my side and glancing at him I thought that I recognised a very famous cinema and radio organist. He was of medium height, had a small, dark, somewhat Hitler-like mustache and looked amiable. I was not sure that he was the man, for I'd only seen a cigarette picture photo of him, but on the other hand if it *was* this organist, I did not want to lose the opportunity of getting his autograph.

Out came my small album, which I always carry around for emergency occasions like this and, lifting my cap, I said to him, 'Please do excuse me, sir. I am an autograph collector – its my life time hobby. I believe you to be someone famous and I would so very much appreciate your autograph. Will you graciously oblige me?' He said that he was not anyone of any consequence. I said, 'Well, if you are not now, I am pretty sure that you will be in a very short time, and so I would like your signature *now* please!' The man shrugged his shoulders, took my book and wrote. 'Suffer little children to come unto *me*. Very truly . . .' and then he signed his name. I thanked him very politely and then Lizzie came up to me as the man walked away. She asked who I'd got and I said that I'd captured the signature of a well-known broadcasting organist. She said, 'Let me see'. We both looked. It was signed, 'Yours truly, Alfred A. Rouse'. *Two years later he was hung for murder.* I saw a facsimile of his writing and his signature in a Sunday newspaper. It was absolutely genuine . . . and I had thought I was getting the signature of Reginald Foort (pray forgive me, Reginald . . . see a photo of this man and you will agree that in the spur of the moment the face could have been yours, and you *could* have been at Southend that evening). Well, there I had a murderer's autograph – just a mere curiosity.

Then around 1938 I was sent by a fan of mine in America a magazine called *Avocations*, a magazine of Hobbies and Leisure, and within it I found a short par on the strange things people collect, i.e. the ropes that folks have hung themselves with, the millions of pearl buttons a woman owns, and then the fact that a lawyer in the State of New York collected the autographs of *Murderers* only! Now, when you are a hobbyist you help fellow collectors when you are able. I had this autograph of Rouse and I did *not* particully want it, so, care of the mag and the editor, I sent it to the lawyer, together with cast iron proof that it was authentic, and said I'd take anything in the way of an autograph of some one reasonably well known as a friendly swop and would not argue over the rate of exchange, as I was doing this in the spirit of international good will. Quite four months of silence elapsed and then out of the blue came from New York a friendly letter and the swop – a line of music from *Ninon* by Tosti who wrote

Goodbye, plus his full signature and date, December 1st 1898. I was very well satisfied.

In the year 1951 I had a very delightfull gift from a *Saturday Book* reader, Mrs Masterman. She sent a letter saying that she was clearing out some papers and came upon a small Chesterton relic in the form of some verse and sketches that he'd done when on a visit to her home. She said that her husband and G.K.C. had been very good friends. She did not want it, nor any money for it, it was a gift in exchange for much laughter given to her via my writings. Would I accept it? I would and did. Two very amusing sketches plus twelve lines of verse all in pencil and all done by Chesterton and a treasure.

I have another literary treasure amongst my souveniers, an I.O.U. signed by Oscar Wilde to More Adey. It was a gift to me from the Rector of Bloomsbury in appreciation of the many smiles my first *Diary* gave him. I have always admired the writings of Wilde, and when G. B. Stern awhile ago asked me to name the greatest British writer of the past 100 years, I named Oscar Wilde. She said that he was what they called an 'ornamental writer' and I said I'd sit in peace on the *same mantlepiece* – and she said that was very witty of me and the sort of thing Wilde would probably have said! I do not care the slightest about a man's moral behaviour – there are plenty of odd freaks in the modern world of literture and Art. In the end its his work that matters and if I could write a play the equal to *The Importance of Being Ernest* I would be very proud of myself.

I really Must tell you that when *Lady Windermere's Fan* was revived at Haymarket Theatre awhile ago I went

round to the stage door to try to find Cecil Beaton or
Oliver Messell, who had both had a hand in this glorious
production. I failed to find them or get their autographs
but since I have got Messell at *The Little Hut* first night
and my kind friend Derek Adkins obtained Beaton's autograph for me. By my side was a chap aged about sixteen.
I chatted with him – asked who's signature he was waiting
for – Oscar Wilde's? He just would *not* believe that Wilde
was dead and said that I was only trying to put him off.
He got quite nasty. I went inside the stage door to get out
of the chap's way and there I met a pal and I told him
about the chap waiting for Oscar Wilde's autograph. My
friend went out and the conversation went like this: 'I
understand, my dear young fellow, that you are wanting
my autograph?' 'Golly, are *you* O. Wilde?' 'I am indeed
Wilde.' 'Sign *Please*, mister', and mister signed. Then the
chap popped his head inside the stage door and said, 'Yer!
Think I'm Potty? I knew there was such a bloke. I've got
him now and you ain't!' And I *hadn't* untill the Rector of
Bloomsbury obliged me.

Although, naturally, I enjoy getting autographs of the
famous personally and having a chat as well, there are times
when it's not possible, and *not* all the famous are obliging.
Paderwiski was a real tarter and seldom obliged. This
pianist had a Cast Iron alibi. Before a concert he would say,
'My hands, my hands, I must rest them' . . . and refuse to
sign, and after a concert he would say, 'My hands, my
hands, they are so tired', and refuse to sign his name. Well,
I reckon that over a period of seven or eight years I must
have asked him so very politely at least a dozen times. It
was not, I will frankly admit, that I admired him as a pianist

(there were many far greater, even at his best) but he was in himself a great man, a patriot. On the very last occasion I asked him and he refused, there happened to be a woman at his side who said to me, 'Haven't I heard you ask before?' I admitted it was probally my 12th refusal from Paderwiski. The woman said that such persistance deserved a better fate. By this time the pianist was in a huge car with another man and the crowd waved as they drive away.

'If you would care to come with me I will give you a signed photograph of Paderwiski. It's rather large and framed and glazed. But it's got a nice inscription.' 'Golly,' said me, 'That would be real spiffin.' She did not know what spiffin ment. I had to explain. We went to flats nearby. Up we went to the second floor. She opened the door and there upon the wall of the hall were three photos in frames. Chaliapin the bass, Tettrazini, the nightingale with a big bust, and Paderwiski, with a long inscription: 'To my dear governor, Mr Aldington and to his dear governor, May Aldington with affectionate greetings' and then fully signed. The lady took it off the wall and gave it to me. I asked if *she* was Mrs Aldington, to which she replied, 'No, I bought it at a jumble sale.' I thanked her very truly and made my way home with a hugh photograph. Not a soul stopped me (not even the police) but I must have looked odd walking down the road with that frame clasped to my little chest. I never saw the kind stranger again. When Paderwiski died in June 1941 I draped that photo with a black tie, not so much in memory of the pianist but in memory of a kind-hearted stranger who made my wish come true.

Amongst my souveniers are some nice Maugham items.

A spotless new second impression of *Liza* signed 'For Fred (his to keep) W. Somerset Maugham'. He gave me that in 1929. He was at my home. He'd signed fourteen first editions for me to sell, and into which he'd put extra long inscriptions, and then from a brown paper parcel he brought out this mint *Liza of Lambeth*. He said, I'm going to sign this one so that you won't sell it. Let it be a souvenier of our friendship for all time. I guarded that copy more than anything else all through the blitz. Still in mint state. Still have it in my personal library.

Then I have *The Narrow Corner* by him, autographed, 'A Christmas present to Fred Bason from W. Somerset Maugham, December 1932'. I was once offered twelve pounds for this copy but glad to say I resisted the temptation. Money ain't everything. I would have to be desperatly up against it before I'd part with any of the souveniers I have written about.

Funny things a born collector collects. At the age of *one* I was given a teddy bear. I still have it. I was a bit of a boy when Pavlova gave me two lillies from her bouquet. I pressed them and still have them. The first love letter I ever got – I was 15 – still amongst my souveniers. *Robinson Crusoe* given as a school prize to my Dad in February 1878, given to me by him on my sixth birthday and started my love of books, I still have it in 1953. A Valentine given me at 18 and the piece of ribbon that was round the cake at my 21st birthday party, I have them. Sentimental me? So what? Perhaps a bit more sentimentality and a little less hardness in this world and it would be a much more pleasant place.

I wonder what my wife will do with all my treasures on

the day I find one decent woman who does not think I am a freak and who will understand or at least try to understand my reason for keeping all these and a thousand other things? Will she say I am your only treasure now and as I can't keep all these things clean and tidy, we must have a glorious spring clean and get rid of the lot? If she says that, we shall have a very glorious bust up, I promise her that – for I have a very good reason why I keep these things around me. They are my childhood, boyhood and the days of my teens and when I bring them out I can and *do* recapture the lost years and they keep me young at heart. All too soon we grow up. All to soon we have to get out in the world and dig for a living.

Memories are very precious to me. I open the drawers of my chest, handle the photos given to me by Ella Shields, Hetty King, Ella Retford, Madeliene Carroll. I get out the fighting photos of Jack Dempsey, Mickey Walker, Jack Hood, Dave Crowley. I look at the sketches of themselves drawn by George Robey and Harry Lauder. I handle the ballet shoe of Vera Nimchinova (what a beauty she was) and Anton Dolin's shoe when he was practically unknown. I look at Rachmaninoff's autograph and recollect the trouble I went to get it, and one of the first photos Gracie Fields ever gave to a fan. And there is my own photo taken at the age of seven, and what a saucy little bloke I looked then.

These are not things which have much commercial value but to me they are priceless. I shudder to think what will happen to them when I am no more upon this earth of ours. What will happen to the letters from D. H. Lawrence, Kathrine Mansfield and E. M. Forster, plus the orig sketches from Lovet Fraser's wonderfull pen? – all of which Michael Sadleir gave to me as a Christmas gift. I would hate to see them go to ashes. I must do something about it. I have made one gentleman's arrangement with Jon Pertwee. If he dies before me I am to have his collection of fancy waistcoats – not that a single one of them will fit me – and he's to have the pick of my autographed photos if he outlives me. I reckon as how I'd better make some other arrangements, but right now I am far too busy living 24 hours a day to think about anything else and as I write this, diary, I am feeling very fit. Remarkably fit when you come to consider that last night I danced three quarters of the time from ten untill five at the Chelsea Arts Ball with a girl, Pamela Nichols, who I think may someday become a great artist. Well, it's about time I had a protege and discovered someone and made them famous – as I have frequently been discovered in my time. My time! Cor, it sounds as if I have finished, when, blow me, I am still only just started. Liz has just brought in kippers all hot and now I gives me attention to kippers and leave my diary for this day January the first – and I have *no* new year resolution to make as I always break them! Well, I must have no secrets from my Diary so I suppose the real resolution must be put down – find a *Mrs* Bason who will let me keep my treasures as well as her.

¶ *January 2nd 1952. After the Ball: A Broadcast in Woman's Hour*

I've got the morning after the night before feeling. I've been *out* all night. What's more I've been *up* all night.

Been to the Chelsea Arts Ball, for the first time in me life. I've had a spiffin time. Best party I've ever been to. I didn't pay to go in, and I did not slip in by the back entrance either. I was a guest of the Director of the ball, yes *me*. Now, if you happen to know me, then you also know that Chelsea *Art* and *Me* are in *No* way related. I was therefore astounded when the Director called at my home in Walworth. He said that as my books had made him laugh he thought it was up to him to give me a night out as a reward – and what a night its been. Cor! I'll tell you all about it, if I can keep from falling asleep.

I went there alone. The resolution that I made on this programme exactly one year ago this very hour about finding a nice young lady for company has not yet come true, so I went alone. But never for a moment did I feel lonely – there was so much to see and never a dull moment. I got there at eleven o'clock. I went there direct from seeing a pantomime. There was a lot better pantomime at the Albert Hall and the four thousand people there made a wonderfull cast for an amazing show. The Theme of the Ball was Huntin', Shootin' and Fishing.

What did I wear? Well, seeing as how it was the first fancy dress ball of my life, I think that I put up a pretty good show. I borrowed one of my landlady's dresses – a flaming red one – and on it I sewes white linen patches. And on each patch I painted with black ink a Danger Sign, like *Wet Pain*, *Mind the Steamroller*, *No Fishing Allowed*, *Mad Dog*, *Don't Hunt* and *Mind the Lights*. The whole dress back and front was covered with don't do this and don't do that. But *me*, Cor luv a duck, I did all the things that me patches said *Don't Do*. I fished for dance partners and I hunted for autographs. Eat a great deal of lovely food as well. I only had three drinks. I could easily have had three dozen. I kept sober. I also kept reasonably alert untill five this morning when we all called it a day.

The nicest thing that I got at the Ball were three phone numbers – yes, three – from ladies who said that they had seen me on television and were pleased to see me in person. Of course, they might only have been saying that to be kind, but anyrate they gave me their phone numbers quite unasked – and there is *no* knowing where they may lead to, is there? I thought that I should feel like a fish out of water in the huge crowed there, but I met some very nice people. And not a soul wanted to talk about *art* to me. There just wasn't time in any case. Three dance bands played all the time, except when art students did their stunts of a grand parade of scenes that must have taken them months to make.

As a guest it was my priviledge to sit in the Director's private box from time to time and view the whole show from a more comfortable position for it became very crowded on the dance floor. From the box I could see how very carefully the whole annual event is planned. Nothing was left to chance. The procession of tableus was an unforgetable sight. And the fancy dresses were very colourfull. No one had a dress like mine. But there seemed to be hundreds of fishermen there. The most original costume was that of a Robot man who had painted himself in silver and by some clever device his eyes lit up. Several people were lit up in another way – but there were no unruly scenes.

Mere words cannot really describe this wonderfull Ball.

Although the entrance fee was three guineas per head, I am very sure that everybody got very good value. Everybody agreed that it was a better ball than the one last year. Of course you could not but notice that a good deal of huntin' and fishin' in the romantic way went on. But it was all good clean fun. Personally I would have found a more comfortable place to do a little courtin' than on cold stone steps in very draughty corridors. But a nice time was had by all. Such a do as this is very good for the morale. We may all have to face hardships this year, but for my part I shall have last night's ball to look back on. Indeed it's an event that will go into my diary so that I always remember it. And to think that I have always lived in London and this was my first visit to the Chelsea Arts Ball. Well, it was all a smashing treat for me. I don't know if I shall ever go again. Who of us really knows what the future holds for us? But if I ever *do* go, then I will most certainly take my own dance partner with me, cause it's *not* really fair to borrow some one else's girl, especially when he's paid sixty-three shillings for her company.

PS A week later. All the three phone numbers proved duds! The ladies were not at home to me. They'd sobered up.

¶ *Sunday January 25th 1952. Midnight.*

Before I say me prayers and lay me down to sleep I really have to write this, for I think it's rather funny. I only had one invite at Xmas, and that was to see a lady in Pimlico the first Sunday after Xmas, but I was so very ill that I could not even get out to phone her, or even write a card that would reach her in time, so it all had to go by till I was well again. Well, I made that visit this evening. I had been invited to see some old theatre programmes which the lady said were not the slightest use or interest to her and that I could have the lot for the calling. Now I do like old programmes when they are very old, i.e. early 18th and early 19th century for they are curious and although I do not sell them, I do at times swop them with collectors either for autographs, cig cards or stamps, so as to have things to swop with others. That's how the hobby world goes round. Well, I get to Chichester Street – that's behind Dolphin Square – about around five o'clock. There was a nice fire burning and tea was all laid out, for I'd told her rain or fine, fog or snow, I would be there for sure and certain, if I was alive. We chatted for half an hour on the weather and the situation in general (which general I forget) then we had tea, and I was given real lovely chicken sandwiches, for the lady said I looked as I needed fatting up (I always do). Then we have super pastry, cherry, jelly tart, then we had mince tart, and then she brought out chocolate ecclairs which she said she'd had made very specially for me. (Reading in my diary, I liked 'em, which is very true, but I was by then absolutely full up and even for fourpence I could *not* have eaten them there ecclairs. So she said I was to take them home. At first I protested but she seemed as if I would offend with too much refusal, as she never eat such things, and so I agreed.)

Well, we then talked for about two hours about people, from H. Beerbolm Tree to W. Macqueen Pope, who she longed to meet, and I said for such a feed I am blooming sure he'd come for a chat, as you are indeed both great theatre lovers. Then we got on to plays and to radio, on and on. The conversation went with a swim as if we had known each other all our lives (I am a pretty good mixer, even if I have to say it myself). Then the ladies daughter came in and she talked first about Joan Hammond, the singer she'd just heard that day and then about Switzerland and the Rambles club and hostels and the cheap way to travel, on and on just as if we'd been pals for years. And then telling me she was a nurse, we had to talk about hospitals. The time speeded by. I looked up and it was near eight. I just had to get home, for I had another engagement. So I got my coat on and the lady put the ecclairs in a tin with other high class pastry to fatten me up, and the daughter put on her coat to see me out to the bus and then she was going to a jazz concert. We got up the road and she said, 'I suppose you have the theatre programmes?' 'What programmes?' says I. 'Well, blow me,' she said. 'The ones you came especially to collect. That's *why* you came.' And do you know, diary, that in the whirl of such varied conversation and a grand tea and two such nice ladies, I'd forgotten every word about the programmes – gorn right out of my head, even though we'd spoken a great deal about the stage in its many aspects. Its the first time I recall in 25 years that this has happened. Last time was when I went to breakfast (yes, breakfast) with Sapper, so that he could autograph some copies of *Bulldog Drummond* and we chatted for an hour on boxers and boxing as we eat, and I walked out of Half Moon St and with the books unsigned under my arm – had forgotten to ask him to do the one thing I'd gone at nine in the morning to get done. Well,

E

the nurse did laugh as she said, 'Now you have a lovely excuse to return for more ecclairs'. But blow me, it was programmes I wanted, not a bilous attack.

¶ *1952*

I saw a delightfull musical picture today called *An American in Paris* with Gene Kelly and a lovely girl called Leslie Carron in the leads. I had a rather lovely girl with me for company. She is exactly one inch taller than me in her shoes, and I would say two inches shorter without her shoes. I shall never see her with her shoes off because three times during the show she called me *Little One* when she spoke, and there is nothing whatever romantic about being called Little One, not even in a most enduring and charming manner. So I will gracefully retire from this ladies company and let her find her big big cave man and she can call him Big One.

¶ *January 1952*

I have written to a magazine which is issued solely to the managers of cinemas a suggestion that I think it would be a really nice thing if they could somehow or other open their cinemas for an occasional morning matinee solely for the blind folks. I have even volunteered to go to any cinema in London to stand on the stage and do a running commentary of the parts of the talkies that cannot be actually followed by the talk. I do feel that the Moguls of Wardour might do something about this. I have further made the suggestion that *no* child under the age of 15 should *ever* be allowed alone into *any* cinema after six thirty at night. Times and times again I have seen hundreds of workers standing in queues outside around seven at night and with little hope of getting a seat when they eventually get inside because children are seeing the show for the second or third time. I feel that by the prior to six or not at all rule for children there might be a few seats for the workers after their day's work.

¶ *November 1952*

This evening I met Pat Wallace (the daughter of the late and ever great Edgar Wallace) for the first time and I told her of a personal recollection of her dad. It's worth telling twice, so I put it down right now. I had been to the Apollo Theatre to see a thriller called *The Man Who Changed His Name* and I found this play a real stinker. Thinking rightly that I had not got value for the price of my gallery seat, I went round to the stage door to collect a few autographs, as it happened to be the first night. Out came the author of it, Edgar Wallace, and although I had his autograph already I thought that I would get it again because it happened to be a very swopable one. He asked me if I had enjoyed the play and I told him that it smelt and that on merit it would not run a week. 'Nonsense,' he said. 'It will run months on my name alone.' 'Then all the more shame for that,' I said. 'Anyrate, I think it's a very poor play and what is more I am willing to bet 2s 6d against a book of yours signed by you that it won't run a week.' 'Done,' said Wallace. We shook hands on it (he had a very clummy soft hand). The play was taken off after four nights. Now I am not the sort of bloke who gloats over the misfortunes and mistakes of others and I did not hurry around seeking out Wallace in order to say to him, 'There, I told you so, didn't I?' It also happened that I had bought up a vicar's library of some five thousand vols and was busy for several weeks sorting and cleaning them – he collected books but he never dusted them – and it must have been all of five weeks before I met Edgar Wallace at another first night. I said to him, 'Sorry about that awfull play, sir. Hope you did not lose too much money'. He looked at me steady for a moment and then said, 'I had a bet with you, didn't I sonny?' 'Yes sir – but it really don't matter.' 'A bet is a bet,' he replied. 'Book against 2s 6d – that's right?' I nodded. 'Come with me,' he said. We went to his big car and from a pocket in the door, he pulled out a copy (1st ed) of *The Flying Squad* – one of his best thrillers – and upon the endpaper he had written 'You Win', and signed his name. He'd carried that book around for a month looking for me.

¶ *November 1952*

It's really funny how at time things stare you in the face and you don't see them, so very obvious only you don't realise it. I am on my way back from giving a lecture at West Bromwich, and I won't ever forget that lecture because on my way there I had a meal on the train and I eat a bit of pie crust and it broke my front two bottom row teeth. They was bad, I will admit, but blow me, not all that bad, and so I had to lecture for an hour with a sort of lisp and a gap in me mouth what I was not used to and which made me feel very self conscious all the time I was on the platform. They were all very nice about it and the talk went down ok and I sold five copies of *Diary Two* completely unasked and unexpected as well, for I'd been told that they were all poor in that town and in any case would not want a Cockney's books, hence I only took six with me. To sell five was proof that I was alright, lisp and all. Well, that's not want I really want to record, diary – it's this. On the train a soldier loaned me a copy of *Weekly Overseas Mail*, November 13th to 17th issue, and I gives him an American thriller that Beatrice had sent me, for it only had one murder in it and that was not a very juicy one at that. I read an article that's all about Chung Ling Soo. Now he was William Robinson and one of the greatest magicians of his day. Although English, he was more Chinese than any Chinaman and even refused to speak English and when dressed up you or anyone would swear *on oath* that he was a Chinaman. Now I have to go back to 1918.

I am eleven and have all the cheek in the world. I have a pal named Bert Fisher and he is on the stage in The Carrie Laurie Juvenile Troup. Bert is me boyhood pal and me hero. He's on the stage; I'd like to be but not got the voice. I follows him around. I think that he's at Wood Green that week and over I goes from Walworth to Wood Green which is a very long way but I am used to long ways and very good on me plates of meat (feet). Well I gets me over there and I find that Bert is not on the Bill – but there is Chung Ling Soo. I waits a long time. All the acts are in but one, and as none looks a bit Chinese I still waits, for by the laws of elemination the last one to go on, if it's not a stage hand or a fireman, must be the star. Eventually I finds this Mr Robinson. I asks. He shakes his head. I stand in the way and asks again. He says nothing. I tells him that I've come miles and miles from Walworth. I might as well have said Wellington for all he cared. We gets nearer the stage door. I almost *begs*. No Bert, and now no autograph. Nothing for a five mile walk. I reckon as how I must have very nearly cried out my last ernest request. He takes my book and he writes: Chung Ling Soo in sort of Chinese Lettering and then puts William E. Robinson beside it, both names Longwise down the sheet in my album. As he hands it back he looks sad and says '*last time*'. I don't know what he means, so I says nothing except thank you and go my weary way back home, a very satisfied autograph collector. I'd got some one – *some great*. He was my 16th capture. The number as I record this is 11,171. What a lot of folks I've met in the past 33 years and what fun as well I've had. No regrets at all. Well, now, at the close of the article I read Chung was disappointed in love. Just before his death he had been turned down by a dark haired American beauty. An examination of the rifle revealed that someone had tampered with the safety catch which held the bullets in the gun. Chung was killed on the stage of the Wood Green Empire whilst doing the spectacular trick of catching bullets fired from a gun. His friends F. Oursler and Will Goldston believe that he committed the most ingenious and cold blooded suicide ever planned, because of a broken heart. He died the night *after* I got his autograph. He said *last time* to me. I know now *why* he said that and do agree that it was planned suicide of a very brave man. He did it himself and knew what would happen. Two live bullets were put into a gun. The assistant fired the gun, but the bullets were held by a safety catch. As the rifle went Bang, Chung had to touch a secret spring behind a plate held in his hands, and two bullets dropped on to the plate and looked as if the magician had caught those bullets in mid air on to the plate. But that night in March 1918 the bullets left the gun and shot Chung through the heart. The coroner's verdict was *Misadventure*. But now I know about the jilting and remember him saying *last time*, meaning last time he would ever sign an autograph album, I agree with the other gent that it was cool calculated suicide and that Chung lost the safety catch that night. What a spectacular death. Cor, it makes you think.

¶ *November 23rd 1952*

Sometimes you can go scatty trying to help folks and blow, the more you try the less they appreciate? I had heard what a very tough job it was and is for an unknown artist to get 'a break' and really earn a living wage from his or her painting for the first few years unless a miracle of good luck comes their way.

I said to myself that I would find just one really talented and completely unknown artist and I would write some articles and then get the unknown to illustrate them, forming with her a gentleman's arrangement and agreement that if I liked the work of hers and it was in keeping with my writings, I would *not* sell my articles to any mag *unless* the editor bought the unknown's pictures that went with it at a very fair price or unless they gave us a fair united sum, then I should share it 60 per cent for my article and 40 per cent for her illustrations, which I deem fair by any standard and indeed liberal terms for any absolutely unknown artist.

I went to an Art School and saw the principal. To him I fully explained my quest and he happened to be a fan of mine and knew all about me. It was plain sailing, he said, and he'd very soon get a nice girl on those terms for me. I said I was not looking for someone to hold my hand but an illustrator for my work and when I found the right one I should make her famous inside two years and she'd have plenty of work in no time, and make good honest living from her art. He quite understood.

I waited. A week later a name and address was given to me. The girl was 20 and talented. Had never sold and was willing to illustrate and was quite agreeable to the terms. I took her places, I introduced her to very famous folks. I gave her a very good time and I did not hold her hand. I begged her to draw a picture of my Westmoreland Road where I've lived all my life. I would write an article on Walworth. O.K. she'd do it. I go to a show, I take her. I want a rough sketch of me in a stage box. O.K. she'd see about it. This all happened in November. January the 28th of the next year she has still not put pencil to paper.

Then I learn – and I am too astounded to make a remark – no she doesn't want to do pictures which any one asks her to do. But only those she *feels* she *must* do in her heart. If she becomes well-known by her own work her own way, so well and good, she don't want to be famous. She wants to do just her own work her own way. She is, I find, in a hell of a job with two halfpennies for wages . . . and she has Talent. Tomorrow, I am going back to the principal of the art school to tell him he ain't a very good picker, but he can try again if he wishes. Meanwhile I will take *art lessons* in all its branches so if some bloody fool of a girl cannot see a honest endeavour to be helped along the road, or just wants to draw that which she feels in her own heart must be drawn and not what a writer needs illustrating, then I will do the blooming illustrations myself – and just find a girl to hold my hand, so help my Bob... or rather so help me ART.

Do my fellow bookmen corner books? Of course they do. I have done it myself – twice. Once I made a very handy sum when I re-sold my stock of Maugham's novels, retaining only those which had very personal inscriptions. But when I re-invested the money by buying, in the first and limited editions, the writings of Martin Armstrong, I very soon found that I had burnt my fingers. And lost my money, for when I tried to re-sell I had to take much lower prices than they had cost me.

It taught me a lesson never again to invest in an author but only in a book. By that I mean give fifty pounds hard cash for a fine copy of *Of Human Bondage* and then put the book away in your bottom drawer until you can get the best price possible over that fifty pounds. Invest in the first book by W. B. Yeats but do not attempt to buy a complete set of the first editions of Yeats or you will surely burn your fingers.

I have never found any real pleasure in book-collecting although I've collected since 15. The only two things which have really given me pleasure in the world of collecting have been autographs and cigarette cards. What fun it was to acquire fifty cards to complete one series! It took ages. Of course one could have gone to a dealer and bought the needed cards. But that would not have been fun.

Some things are nicer the harder they are to obtain. How I would like a nice signed photo of Greta Garbo. Her autograph is very scarce because she is unco-operative and lacks amiability to collectors. Hence, what fun to be the one to get it – from her – instead of paying 25s (as was offered to me in 1951) for a signed photo of her. I would get no kick out of paying a thousand for a short letter from Abraham Lincoln, but I would get a thrill standing beside Eisenhower for a moment and getting him to write his name in my album. To write an important letter to old man Churchill and get a reply from him would be a means of getting his signature; but I got more fun out of being refused with a wave of his hand and a cheery smile. We who collect this and that and the other may be weird folks, but thank goodness we are happy ones.

¶ *1952*

A letter from me was chosen and read out on the very first edition of 'Dear Sir', the justly popular B.B.C. programme, because the producer of it specially wrote to me asking me to as it were start the ball rolling. My letter said that *no* paid newspaper or journal theatre critics should be allowed to attend a new show in their official capacity untill the *third* night so as to give the players every possible oppotunity to be word perfect and the producer the chance to make minor changes. I think this is a sane suggestion and so did many of the listeners who wrote me. But still, and I expect for ever more, critics will attend the first night.

Once I offered to lecture at my local public library on the pitfalls of beginner authors – for nothing, and got a sneer and we've got no room here for *such* things. And the very next night I talked at Tottenham Public Library at a high fee on the same theme! Of course, I would never again offer to speak in Southwark. Why my goodness, diary, the only poor and downright unkind reception I've ever had in twelve years of public talking came from The Southwark Rotary Club. Yes, my local club. Yet a week later I was a great hit at Luton Rotary Club and four days later a success at Leeds Rotary club; which proves that a prophet is *always without honour in his own district*. I begged my local public library to put the jacket of my *Diary Two* in their window amongst the dozens on display and provided one for that purpose. Was it put on display? Oh no of course not. I went past their windows every second day for three months. I know it was *never* put in the window display, yet the local hatters and the local Co-operative stores put my book in their windows! Bless their kind hearts. This sort of thing is heart-breaking to the local author. If I was a writer in Paris they'd be so nice to me. If I lived in Eastbourne, they'd display all my writings. Oh shades of Charles Dickens. They have all your writings, and Shelley and old Bill Shakespeare. Organise a book display in Southwark and you will see *all* of their writings, none of mine. What the hell? Thank God for me fans in Paris, Eastbourne, Tottenham, and, strange as it may seem, in Ilekley as well! Besides Pio Pio (New Zealand), New York and Shanghai.

¶ *December 13th 1952*

Tonight I have listened to *The Return of a Soldier* by John Van Druten from the novel by Rebecca West on the radio adapted by Peggy Wells. I saw this play when it was first produced at The Playhouse theatre in June of 1928. I was in those days a very ardent fan and indeed something of a friend of Mary Clare who was the lead in the play. Often I would pop in after a matinee for a little chat. Mary was always amiable to little me. The play was produced in a very hot summer and it stuggled along for a few weeks to half empty houses and then Mary said that the notices were up and that they feared they would have to close down, it was not paying its way. This news makes me very sad. I have so enjoyed this play. It was sad but it was real. I knew that although *Young Woodley* was making a name for Van Druten he wanted this play to run as well. I knew that Mary Clare loved the play and I also knew that to two in minor roles it ment the world, for it to continue awhile longer. What could I do? What on earth could I do? True, I had even in those days a great many friends and I knew a good many people who really mattered. I could write to them, ask them to help a very worthy cause. *The Return of the Soldier must* run longer, MUST. I had – oh how I remember – just exactly five pounds in the post office bank. I withdrew three pounds of it. I told my mother what I was doing. She said that I was an utter fool but that it was my cash and if I cared to squander it on a whim to help some actors and actresses who would not give me a penny if I was starving and a dramatist who didn't even know me, then it was my own affair. Well, it was my own affair. I wrote letters to St John Ervine, Arnold Bennett, Somerset Maugham, asking them to so kindly tell their friends to see this wonderfull play. I asked James Agate to give to it his second and very important attention. I wrote to several actresses I knew, Mimi Crawford as one, Lyn Harding as another of note whom I asked to say a kind word to their friends and to visit this play if they had the time. Then I went over to the City to a firm called Stevenson who did duplicating and who were nice folks to me. There between us we connocted a letter to the effect that a wonderfull human kindly and finely acted play was going to end through lack of public support. Don't let it happen. It must *not* happen. Oh it was a smashing letter, full of love of theatre. But I think it was (I will confess it now) love of Mary Clare – we are now so old – that made me do this. She was a big strong handsome woman. I was a little bloke, and you do know the fascination of contrasts. Little men always adore *big* girls: oh how she will laugh if she ever reads this. We met in 1951 after not meeting for ten years. She looked in 1951 a little bigger but just as nice as ever. I was still the little bloke. I sent many many dozens of these duplicated letters out, aided by a phone book and I handed others to folks at first nights and concerts and even at boxing matches. The notices came down, the play went on. The notices went up again after a couple of weeks. I sent out more letters and appealed to more folks, including a couple of *lords* whom I am ashamed to say that I knew. The notices came down again as the audiences picked up. The show dragged on and on. A lingering death – and finally it died. But it lived awhile longer than it would normally have done because I, a galleryrite, loved this play and adored the leading lady. All I got was a letter of thanks from Van Druten, when Mary obviously told him – for I had not – and friendship with Mary Clare, which lasted for about two years. And then I found another larger woman to hero worship. But it all came back tonight – 1928-1952 – Oh God, how the years go. What memories of the years between.

¶ *December 16th 1952*

This is a day that I am unlikely ever to forget. I spent several hours on the crack liner s.s. *America* as a guest of the owners. There was a marvellous luncheon which commenced with caviare and vodka and finished with champange and had eight courses of the loveliest food I have ever eaten! – including steak that had to be seen to be believed, and which simply melted into ones mouth with correct steak cooking (done by radar). How did I get on this super liner? How did it all happen? Well, one day Liz said to me, Fred, someday you will get yourself a woman of your own and get you married. Now you will have to have a honeymoon and on the sea would be best for a nice honeymoon. Well, no nasty boat for you, and the misses – the best or *none*. The Best may not be the biggest but how'd you know if the biggest isn't the best unless you try it? s.s. *America* has won the blue ribbon and the papers are full of its wonders. But what of the beds? What about the comfort of the beds? There are two thousand beds on that there boat – are they comfortable? You can't ask the captain. And the owners are sure to say that all the beds are superlatively comfortable. But you take no one's word for comfort, find out for yourself, that's the ONLY way. After all, it is to be your honeymoon, not the captain's. So I went around, not very far, round my files seeking some one who knew someone. You know what I mean. But I was so lucky. I found in my files a fan who held an important position in the company – that's the owners (with the U.S.A. government) – of the wonderfull s.s. *America*. I have ten thousand usefull friends and fans listed in my files and I reckon that between them they could remove mountains for me if I so wished mountains to be removed. A letter to my friend: *are* the beds comfortable? soon brought a letter to the effect that I'd better go and find out. Few more letters to arrange the day of the visit and December 16th chosen. Tickets for me first class provided by the company (they do things in style) in a Pullman train. Coffee and cakes en route. Not knowing what was in store for me I said to the man seated opposite me that I would put one of the cakes in me pocket in case I got a starvation meal on the liner and was hungry soon afterwards. He got a good laugh out of this, but how was I to know? I'd never been on a big boat before in my life. I'd never had American hospitality before. I was a raw Cockney. But I soon learnt. At Southampton we went up an esculator into the heart of the boat. Cocktails and prawns and so many many appitizers that one had a good meal before one had a good meal – and got three parts tight on the liberal amount of drinks – and when you wanted a cigrette you was given a whole packet of Chesterfields. Amazing. (I brought home three half packets.) Luncheon was at one. We guests eat

and eat and eat. I never finished one course – bits of the
eight were enough for me – and I got up from my table
so full up I thought that I would burst. (Greedy guts? Not
really. It would have been down right rude to have refused
something of each course.) I do not know what the other
guests did. Probally found a cabin and sleepted it off. Bell-
boys were at our service together with officers to show us
all over the ship. I did a bit of climbing on to the sun deck,
on to the captain's deck, up to the funnells, but I got a
bit tired of that so I came down and started that which
I'd come to find out, and I went into some 15 cabins and
examined the beds. I had all the close off one bed when
a man who was passing looked in and said 'What flea
hunting already?' I said that I was doing nothing of the
kind and that I was just seeing what sort of springs the
beds had. He then asked if I was in the furniture trade
and was at loss for words when I said I was a bloke what
was searching for a comfortable honeymoon. I laid myself
down on four beds. I examined the sheets and pillows on
the beds on various decks, getting hopelessly lost in the
seeking. But I can now report to my own satisfaction that
the beds on this liner are comfortable. Only thing I did
not find was a *double* bed. And although I am myself a
small bloke and can get into the beds very comfortably,
I don't think there will be room for a reasonably sized
wife in *my* bed. Which would be rather a shame on my
honeymoon since I'd like to sleep with my wife on *that*
occasion.

¶ *December 28th 1952*

I feel very unhappy this Sunday afternoon. Why are women so very unkind? I met a woman in a book binder's office. She looked very sweet. The book binder who is a particular pal of mine obliged me with a copy of Pepys *Diary* so that I could send it out to Sally Purvis in Berlin, who said that she longed to read it. By way of return (for the binder would take no money) I sent to the pretty woman in his office my first diary. She wrote a very friendly letter some weeks later to me and enclosed a photo signed with fond wishes. Seven weeks before Xmas I sent her a new and nicely signed copy of Diary Two. Five weeks before Xmas I sent a letter expressing the hope that she'd received *Diary Two* and that it had pleased her and suggesting that we meet for a nice tea in the West End on December the 28th, which day Lizzie would be out visiting her relations. Or if that failed to please her because of the vile weather could I come to her home, bring with me some tea and sugar (and a box of chocolates) and perhaps she would give me a cup of tea and we could have a little chat, with her mother for chaperone. I got no answer to either the note enclosed in my diary or my friendly letter, so two weeks before Xmas I sent the box of chocolates. I would have taken it over together with a card of Greetings and expressing the hope that nothing I'd said had offended her and *please* would she reply, as now I had an invitation to Pimlico for that December 28th, but so much wanted to meet the handsome lady in the bookbinder's shop. Please reply! Yesterday was Saturday and I must confess that I awaited all the three mails of the day with much more than my usual interest, but no letter from the woman. And by the late mail it was too late to clinch the engagement at Pimlico. So now I am alone this Sunday the 28th December. Parties on both sides of me, music all around and I feel bloody miserable. I have drunk three glasses of port and I put this entry down hardly seeing what I am doing. I do feel a tinge of self pity. I do not know what more I could possibly have done. I gave away a 9s 6d *Diary*. I gave away a 7s 6d box of chocs. I gave them gladly. I only wanted to be friends with the woman in the book binder's shop. I only asked for a 2½d reply.

¶ *1952*

Nancy Spain wrote in her review of my second diary in *The Daily Express* that I seemed to like to make every day a *Red Letter Day*. How very true that is. I like to make every day just a little different from the previous one and in that way I live a full life and enjoy almost every moment of it.

November the 24th, which was a Monday, banished any Monday feeling for on this day I have luncheon at Kettners off the Charing Cross Road – and for the first time ever in my life I had *Turtle Soup*. I believe that the snobs and the so called important people at Guildhall Banquets start with this here soup. Well, they are lucky people if it's prepared the same way as it is at Kettners, for their soup was proper lovely and went down me a treat as it was hot and tasty. And then I had *duck* and green peas. I've had peas lots of time because one of my own very simple luxuries in life is a tin of hot peas all to myself. They gives me wind, but I love 'em. And so I had 'em, wind and all. But this was the first time I'd ever eaten duck. There was a lotta bone but what Duck was there was jolly tasty and I enjoyed it.

This lunch was paid for by my lawyer, Stanley Rubinstein, who was once Jimmy Agate's lawyer (I have not got any law, but I have a lawyer just in case: it sounds so very nice to have a lawyer).

This luncheon was so that Stanley could meet in person Nancy Spain, and I am bound to record that they got on like a house afire, chatting away about this and that. I will not record what this was and I would most certainly never say a word about that. Had I been in a less posh place I am very very sure that I would have picked up that there duck in me fingers and got all the meat off them there bones. After all, it cost a great deal of money and I wanted to have Stanley's monies worth. Yes, diary, he paid the very big bill, big at least as far as my pocket would be concerned.

There cannot be a more generous hearted man in London than Mr Rubinstein. He don't say to me, 'Come to lunch' and then look down the list and say, 'am having fish and chips, that would do you good and it's the cheapest thing on the Bill of Fare'. He don't do anything like that. He just hands the foreign language menu over and you just picks out. Well, diary, you *know* how I picks out what I want. I don't read the blooming things cause I don't know what on earth they stand for. I just reads *the prices*. If there is something at 7s 6d and something at 5s 6d, I of course has the 7s 6d cause Kettners, Verrys or anywhere else would not have the blooming impudence to charge

7s 6d for a thing what was only worth 4s; and it stands to commonsense that the 7s 6d must be pretty good, not only because of its price, but because of the prominance its displayed on the me and you. One of these days I may see meself in the *Ritz*. I hope that I do not there choose something marked 9s and find it's the Head waiter, or something equally startling.

This was a very happy Luncheon. It started at 1.15 sharp and Nancy *had* to go at 2.30 to feed some baby – no, not her own. The mother had the flu and Nancy was turning nurse for old times sake. Stanley and I lingered over wine till 3 and then he had to go back to Grays Inn (I gave him a History of Grays Inn as a little gift).

I went (rather tight I must admit, for I'd had a sherry and three very full glasses of some rich red wine, name and vintage unknown), to David Low, who suggested that a strong cup of tea would probably pull me round. So we had two strong cups of tea in the A.B.C. He thought I was kiddin him when I said that I had had lunch at Kettners. He said that quite important people eat there, and I said, 'Well, David, I am very important people, and what is more I had Turtle Soup.' That stunned him. He had nothing to say and me, I wanted to get to the W.C. and went on my way rejoicing – another a *Red Letter Day*.

¶ *My list of Favourites, 1953*

Favourite Comedians, Bernard Miles Norman Wisdom Max Wall

Favourite Actors, Alec Clunes Frank Pettingell Dirk Bogarde

Favourite Actresses, Flora Robson Evelyn Laye Jane
    Wenham
Favourite Radio Commentator, Richard Dimbleby
Favourite Ballet Dancers, Anton Dolin Beryl Grey M.
    Fonteyn
Favourite Journals, *Esquire, Reader's Digest, Daily
    Express*
Favourite Dream of my Life, A month in America to give
    some lectures!
Favourite Ambition, To own a nice, loyal, amiable wife –
    and a bathroom
      (oh no, there's no connection, I don't want a Bride in
      a Bath!)
Favourite Radio Stars, Dick Bentley Anne Shelton Vic
    Oliver
Favourite Novel in past three years, *Heaven and Herbert
    Common* by F. Tilsley
Favourite newspaper journalists, Nancy Spain, Arthur
    Helliwell
Favourite city of England, Eastbourne

¶ *List of Dislikes 1954*

Starlets who *only* shine in the audiences at first nights
Hereditary titles, especially 'My Lord'
The O.B.E. for no known reason!
The crowds of coloured gents who come from our colonies
    to be supported by us – on the dole and never intend to
    work!
The Pomp and the Ceremony which the so called aristo-
    crats indulge in out of tax payers money

The way that newspapers 'jump on' well known people who do a minor wrong and make them front page news whereas they would have no mention if they were not well known!

The cruelty of government officials who, knowing they *can* make your life hell, *do so!*

The people who send you manuscripts for your opinion and when you give an opinion they tell you you don't know what you are talking about.

The people who invite you to dinner not for yourself but to make up a number or in order to get a free after dinner speech.

¶ *1953, various dates*

This made Arnold Bennett laugh: – On page 27 of my second Diary (*please* don't ask for a free copy) there is a line which caused me to have more letters than anything else I've written in the past three years. The words are: 'Arnold Bennett gave me a present tonight in exchange for a hot joke. (By 'hot' I may say I do *not* mean the temperature of the joke but that it is up to date – i.e. 'red hot news'). Hundreds of people all over the world have asked me to tell them the joke. To save anyone else writing I will put it in print for the final time. There is a lady who is rather unwell so she goes to a Doctor and says, 'I am not well. I'm rather constipated'. The doctor says, 'Well, don't you take anything?' And she replies, 'Oh yes, Doctor, I always take my *knitting!*' This joke slayed Bennett. *Now* are you satisfied.

¶ *Observation*

There is a big craze for women to slim. I think this is silly. I know it's not pleasant for a woman to be like a beer barrell and must be rather uncomfortable for them to go up and down stairs and lace up their boots. But I believe women ought to *look* women and *not* flat-chested rashers of bacon in skirts. Venus was my idea of just about right, but I wouldn't turn down a woman with a stone more here or there. When I see extremely slim women I do not know if they have T.B. or are plain stupid – so I give them a miss. And strangely enough 98% of the time they *are* Miss.

¶ *From a fan in America comes this absorbing tale*

A gentleman in Alabama has just been fined ten dollars. Being keepted awake by his neighbours noisy dog the gentleman sat on his own porch and howled back louder than the dog! I suppose this proves two wrongs don't ever make a right – but it made ten dollars for the U.S.A. Government. My sympathy goes to the man in Alabama. I've often wanted to do this – haven't you?

¶ *A paragraph from my Diary the Day I was 21*

I learn with great interest that Peter the Great used to go to sleep with his head resting on the tummy of a negro. And heaven alone helped that poor coloured man if his tummy pillow moved and disturbed Peter's slumber. I think I would like to try this out once in my life, but *not* with a coloured pillow. I would ever so much like a glamorous film actress because if she had any talent she could control her wind as she controls her emotions and I would not be disturbed as she chews the cud! I am 21 today. I'll make that an ambition. The tummy of a lovely lady for a pillow before I'm 51.

* * *

¶ *January 3rd 1953*

  M. Sadleir, Pett Ridge and S. Aumonier

In the January the third edition of *Time and Tide*, Michael Sadleir reviewed my Second Diary and after giving it considerable praise complained that I had not written anything about W. Pett Ridge, and, except for a tale told to me by Stacy Aumonier, I'd not mentioned him either! He ended the review by saying, 'Please, more thumbnail sketches of individuals'.

I assume that he wants more of Aumonier and something of Ridge; but these men are both very dead and their writings are just as dead as they are. I have no wish to fill my diaries with dull recollections of very dead men when there are much more interesting people and things to write about. But I know that Mr Sadleir is a wise man and I would be a dam fool to utterly ignore his advice. So, for him and for the few who may be interested, I will put on record just two glimpses of these men who were supposed to be Humourists and whom you'd reasonably expect to say something funny.

But did they? Not a bit of it. They were quite serious men. W. Pett Ridge said (and I put it down at once, so

as there would not ever be any mistake), 'I get a great deal
more pleasure from hearing a man playing a mouth-organ
and enjoying doing it, than from listening to a high class
orchestra playing a solumn overture for money'. And
Stacy Aumonier said, 'I look on the spirit of Reasonable-
ness as about the highest ideal of Human Culture'.

Me, I can't see what's interesting in either statement and
I am very sure that, if ever seen in print, they will bore
my readers to tears, and that's a thing I forever wanted to
avoid. Still, I puts 'em down and maybe someday M.
Sadleir himself will see them and be satisfied that I did at
least take some of his advice.

I never heard W. Pett Ridge say a single funny thing.
He was a very kind and good man but outside writing as
far as I knew him he was not a humorist! Stacy Aumonier
could tell a tale very well – he was a recounter (spelt
wrong). Fred Duprez, who was a music hall great teller of
tales in my youth, said that Stacy was his master. But to
look at him you'd have thought that he had all the troubles
of the world on his shoulders. He more often looked sad
than glad and he looked very much what you would think
a man of letters or of the arts looked like. But W. Pett
Ridge, he looked like a dealer in horses!

But oh! How awkward it is to accept and use advice in
the writing of books! Some said of my first diary that it
jumped around too much. Others were pleased with its
surprises of not knowing what would be on the next page.
Some said less Cockney tales and more about the famous.
Others wanted far far less about the famous and lots more
stories. Sadleir advises more thumbnail sketches and some
say a full portrait of one man is far better than bits and

pieces about many. I have myself refused ever to give would-be authors advice upon their unpublished master-pieces. I have found it best to guess the advice that they want, and then give them exactly that. But at times even that fails to satisfy them; and they start arguing, and soon tell you that you don't know what you are talking about, which may be quite true, but you don't care to be told so by someone who has yet to have one piece of work printed and paid for by someone other than themselves. All in all, I think that it's the best thing to listen to advice and then use your own judgement. You can't please everybody, no matter how you try; so its best to please yourself and, if there are in the end some cans to take back, well you can take them back because the fault has been your own.

¶ *Early 1954. The thing to do!*

One of the nicest people I have met in the past three years has been Phyllis Calvert, the film star. We had a pleasant ten minutes chat in her dressing room at The Strand Theatre during the run of *Escapade*. She asked me what I was doing at that moment and I said I was engaged on a series of talks at all manner of clubs (from Rotary to Woman's Institutes) all over England. She said she was often called upon to speak at 'dos' and just didn't know what to say – so I gave her a piece of advice which E. Phillips Oppenheim had given to me more than twenty years ago. It's so good that its worth putting on record for the first time, as it may prove usefull to you, the reader, when you get called upon quite unexpectedly to give a short talk.

You start *very slowly* to get up and as you start to get up you say 'There was an occasion when King Solomon met Cleopatra in the desert under most romantic circumstances and he said to her, "Honey, I haven't come here to talk." Well, like King Solomon, I haven't come here to talk!' And there *you sit down!* You can substitute any names in the headlines of divorce news if you are unwise and brave. But if you are wise as King Solomon you will stick to King Solomon and Cleopatra.

Phyllis Calvert thanked me and said she would use it on *all* future occasions. With that piece of advice on public speaking, I have made a glamourous charming new friend!

¶ *I sees the Point . . .*

From time to time over the past 20 years I had wondered what was the point of a point-to-point meeting. Mark you, the matter had not in any way worried me, because I'd always been given to understand that, for the most part, these meetings were principally attended by the bloods of Society and Society-conscious females. These are classes I don't usually mix with, as we seldome speak the same language. Sometimes in dentists and barbershops I have come upon snooty society mags, in which there have appeared pictures of Lady Hyde Park and The Hon. Victoria Station at Point-to-Point meetings, resting their bottoms upon sticks which have a point at the other end, and I can truly say that I have wondered if they were the points from which such meetings derived their names.

When in 1953 I got an invitation actually to attend a real point-to-point meeting in Warwickshire, I jumped with joy and at once accepted the invitation. After all, when you gets to be forty any fresh experience is very acceptable when it's pleasant; and I was sure this was going to be pleasant, for I was going with a very dear friend of mine, Col. W. E. Lyon, a giant of a man and a very noble gentleman. When I told Liz that I was going to have a Basonfull of point-to-point, she thought I said Pint-to-Pint and she advised me to lay off the wallop. When I clearly said Point-to-Point, she had no idea what on earth such a thing was, but hoped that I would not tear my trousers on the point.

I put on my very best suit for this occasion. But I need not have troubled. Except for my cap (which was perhaps just a little loud for the occasion) I was one of the best dressed blokes at the meeting. I also put on my very best manners. I had no wish to say 'Wot cher, cock' to a bloke and then find out that he was a blooming baronet. Not that it really matters what you says to Baronets these days, when many of them stand at the gates of their stately homes with collecting boxes in their hands so that the likes of me can put in a few bobs and go and inspect their bedrooms, water works and other places of interest. But I have found it wise to do as the Romans do, when I happen to be in Rome.

For the purpose of this meeting I stayed with Col. Lyon at Stow on the Wold. The point-to-point meeting was on Alcester Heath some thirty miles away, and we travelled in a nice car through some very weirdly named places like Moreton on the Marches, Stretton on the Fosse, and I am pretty sure that we passed through Pimples on the Posterior!

Now although we reached the meeting one and a half hours before it was due to commence, there were hundreds of folks there already. They must have been really anxious to lose their money. And by the time the first race started at two o'clock I reckon that there were five thousand people of all classes on that there Heath. We all inspected the courses and of course it was a blooming long walk over very uneven ground, more like a hike than a walk.

At every fence there was stationed three or four first aid and ambulance men with full kit. It looked very forbidding. You'd have thought that there was going to be a blooming *battle*.

Col. Lyon and me had got about a mile along the course, when a man on a lovely grey horse came along and politely asked us if we would chuck any rather large stones we saw *on* the course *off* the course; so of course we tried to oblige him. But I just couldn't see the course between the fences. There were no guides to the width, and I am jolly sure that I wasn't much help and put stones *on* the course when I should have been taking them off. By the time I have travelled the whole of the length of that there course I was feeling very tried, and when we got back to the car I was glad of a nice drop of sherry to fortify me against the rigours of a cruel cold wind that had obviously sharpened itself against ice-bergs on its way from the North Pole to Alcester.

Looking around me as I drank me sherry, I gathered that the fashionable attire at these here 'dos' is a corduroy cap with a small peak, a duffle coat (ex Navy) grey trousers (ex American army) and stout boots (ex Swiss Alps). I do not think that there was any fashion for women,

as none at all seemed in any way smartly dressed – all
dressed for warmth rather than style, and I did not blame
them. As an innocent at his first meeting it was obvious
to me that you have to be very Hardy to follow point-to-
point. One woman, who was pointed out to me as being
extremely wealthy, had on an old felt hat that my landlady would not be seen dead in.

Now we come to the actual racing. Not a favourite won
in the whole meeting. Two odds-on favourites that everyone but me considered to be absolute certs got beaten on
the run-in of the last 200 yards, sort of pipped on the post
and you should have heard the sighs. One horse was ridden
by a real live *lord* and I am sure that it is still running. I felt
that I had to give a sub to the poor bookmakers, and I
invested one shilling on Little Willie at ten to one. The
race started at 2.40. My fancy ought to have started at ten
minutes to one to get round that course by two-forty. It
lost by over a mile, yes, over one mile in a two mile race!
I suggest that they rename it Weary Willie. I was very
interested in an event called The Adjacent Hunts Ladies
Race. I did not of course know the form of either the
horses or the ladies, but I have a good eye for female form,
and so I bet on a lady who had a very nice form that showed
through a maroon sweater. Looking at her I was sure she
would go places. Places she may go in the future; but bai
jove, she went no places on that day. The winner and the
other two placed horses had been unsaddled and folks were
betting on the next race, when she and her horse wandered
in. So I lost another shilling.

All in all the backers at this meeting had a very lean time.
I do not think that one in forty gained any money. But

maybe they didn't mind, and the point was the point of point-to-point and not the money. Although there was *no* charge for admission to the meeting, the afternoon really can be a little expensive. It's by no means a working man's sport unless the working man is very often on time and a half. The race cards cost 2s 6d each, and you just have to have a card in order to see what you are going to *lose* on. There were a great many children there, and they had a lovely time. Well, if you likes noble horses and gallant men and women, riders in gay colours and jockeys' uniforms, its a nice way to spend an afternoon, provided you are well wrapped up.

Now I must tell you something that happened and which I consider funny. For several races I had sat on the top of Colonel Lyons' car in order to get a reasonably good view, but had failed to see more than jockey-caps as they flashed by. I thought it wise to have a *really* first class view of at least one race, for I never have yet written upon something I've not seen. Well, I went down to the course, and there I found a bale of hay besides a low four-wheeled cart. I got on the bale and then onto the cart, and was joined by several children. I shared out some sweets and we all became pals, although they could see that I was a foreigner. We had a very clear view of at least three hundred yards of the course. Presently up come three women accompanied by a very natty gentleman, with an old school tie. The four of them gets on the cart with me and the kids, and there I am, very happy and contented. The race begins and I gets up and does a bit of shouting: 'Go on something! Go on something!' I have no money on the race, so it don't matter to me what horse wins. The race is nearly over and the horses are in the last two hundred yards, when the natty gent next to me on the cart says most politely: 'Would you care to move a little to one side if you please?' I says: 'Why, mate? You can see over my little head ... can't you?' He says: 'I happen to be the *judge*, and I should like a *clear* view of the course' ... So of course I moves aside ... even I can realise that the Judge really ought to have a view so that he can see what wins the blooming race ... he was very nice about it ... and so I hope was I, 'obliging me'. I had wondered why there had been a flag pole with a Union Jack so gallantly waving on it just beside the cart. I was sure they had not put up that flag for *me*, but I had *no* idea that it was the Judge's stand. All in all a nice experience.

¶ *March the 10th 1953 at Midnight*

Tonight has been an experience. I have spoken to the Young Israelites of Ilford, a youth club of Jews around the ages of 16 to 25. For around three-quarters of an hour I held their complete attention and made them laugh with me and never at me. I did not make any charge when I accepted this engagement because I had never before spoken to an all Jewish audience, and when one makes an experiment one should pay for it and not expect to be paid. But when it was over, in a very nice way, they gave me ten and six-pence and as it was given so nicely, I accepted it in the same spirit.

Now I know that I can hold almost any audience, for these were all lively young people and I am very sure that they would not have sat listening to a Cockney unless he was very amusing or very interesting. A photographer was there and I had my photo taken signing autographs for my audience. They actually *asked* for autographs and I wrote on most of the bits of paper: 'With pleasure...if you are not kiddin me, Fred Bason'. I really enjoyed myself. Indeed I am sure that we *all* enjoyed ourselves, especially a young lady in the front row who laughed and laughed till tears came into her eyes, and I had to warn her in case she P.d herself and that made her even worse. Oh yes, we had lots of fun and I am to revisit them a year hence.

The secretary drove me to Gants Hill station and I had to wait ten minutes for a train. I sat down between two people, both of whom were reading. Out of sheer curiousity I gazed at their reading material (a bookseller always does) and the lady on my left was reading *The Power and the Glory* by Graham Greene. The man on the other side was reading my first Diary. I stared at it. Then I looked at him and I said, 'My Goodness' right out loud. He looked at me, then back at the book. I said nothing. He looked back. I grinned. He said, 'My Goodness – is it possible?' I said that it was not only possible but was happening right there and then. 'I wrote that book and I do hope that you are enjoying it'. He that he was that, it was a real delight and what was I doing over in his part of the world? I told him of the Young Israelites, of Ilford. He said, 'MY Goodness' again, and added that his daughter was in that audience and belonged to that club. I did not dare ask him what size his daughter was in case it turned out to be the stout wench who'd sat in the front row and laughed herself to tears.

He wanted me to sign the copy he was reading, but it

F

turned out to be public library copy and I did not wish to get fined for damaging public property. I signed my name to a statement on one of his old envelopes to the effect that I'd sat at his side whilst he was reading my first diary. He was very nice. Gave me a good grade cigarette and was interested to know I was now at work on my third Diary. The train came in. We sat together for two stations and parted like good friends. I forgot to ask his name. Ships that pass in the night.

¶ *March the 7th 1953*

Before I go to bed, my Diary, I must record an adventure which may never be read by anyone but as you know that never worries me. Perhaps the only consolation I've had from my bit of fame in the past few years are the generous invitations I've had from such nice people to spend weekends in their homes at the seaside or country so as to get a break form the foul air of my own slum Walworth. Most invitations I accept with deep and sincere gratitude (and I always take some food or gifts so as never to impose or cadge.) Well, Diary, you alone know when I am not away for the weekend I go out on my own on the Saturday exploring some part of my London so I can be a good guide to any overseas fans when they visit me. Today being Saturday and me having nowhere particular to go this is what I did and just what happened.

I dressed myself tidily and made my way over Westminster Bridge for a walk to Shepherd's Bush via Oxford Street and the Bayswater Road. I did not hurry. When a shop window attracted my attention I paused and gazed at

the things for sale. I read posters and all manner of adver-
tisements. Looked at the stills in cinemas : and several times
went into shops to ask the prices of unmarked things in the
windows – out of sheer curiousity and without the slightest
intention of buying them. For instance I enquired at a
jewellers the price of a handsome engagement ring. It was
one hundred and fifty-six pounds. I was tempted to ask if
they threw in a woman as well at that price, since I had no
woman to buy it for. But it was a smart shop and they might
not have seen the funny side of my polite enquiry.

I had long passed Marble Arch and was a good way
along the Bayswater Road –indeed within two hundred
yards of Notting Hill Gate. It was exactly 2.30 p.m.
and the sun was shining brightly. Suddenly a youngish
lady with very high heeled shoes and expensive nylons
stopped me. 'Hello, dearie', she said. 'Would you like to
come along with me? Only two pounds for the whole
afternoon. You can have my mate –look, she is just across
the road –for an extra thirty shillings. We will give you
very good value. You look nice. It will be nice for *all* of
us'. This she said without a single pause. I think I must
have shown my feelings in my eyes. 'Look at the sunshine',
I said. 'I've come out for *sun,* not *sex.* Don't you think
you'd better enjoy the sun as well? There is a time for
everything – and not at 2.30 on a lovely afternoon. Are you
broke? Did you have a bad night's trade last night?' 'No',
she had a good night. But business was business and, if you
have a good afternoon's work, then you don't have to go
out at night, and she thought it was going to be a wet night
and she had a bit of a cold on her, see?

She was very matter of fact. It was all sheer business

with her. I said that I thought she might do something better with her life. She said that making men happy, even at a price, was a pretty good thing to do. I had no answer to that. She asked for a cigarette and I gave her one. She lit it with a very expensive lighter – a gold one I am sure, and it had an American eagle on its side. Which American had she stolen that from? What mug had gone home with her and been robbed.

She did not thank me for the cigarette and I was just going when she asked me for half a crown. I said, 'What the hell for?' She said for the cheap thrill of talking to her and for wasteing her valuable time. I said *cheap* was *right*, but thrill there wasn't, that I was *not* a twirp but a born Londoner, and what did she want to make of it? She looked at me as if she was going to make something of it, so I pulled my cigarette from her lips stamped on it, gave her a horse's laugh and walked away. She said something and if I had caught what it was, maybe I'd have gone back and had a lovely row with her. God help any visitor to the Coronation who comes into her sweet and gentle claws! At Notting Hill I got on a bus to Shepherds Bush where I called on my bookselling friends in the market. They were delighted to see me and we had a nice chat. After some tea, I walked back the way I'd come and was near Queens-way tube station, when I was asked, 'Like a little time with me? Only two pounds. Do you good. You can have my mate as well for another thirty-five shillings. Both of us will make you happy. She's just across the road'. Lo and behold, although at least two hours had passed, I'd bumped into the girl who'd been across the road on my outward journey, only this one wanted an extra five shillings for her mate. I shook my head. But *why* the extra five shillings? Diary, I hadn't the guts to ask that woman why their tariffs had not agreed. Well, that's what happened. Another side of life in London.

¶ *March 18th 1953*

I feel a bit browned off and no little bit angry today. Last month I got an extreemly pleasant letter from a reader in Surrey. Much praise for my diaries and would I care to come down to her home for a week-end in June and talk to her young Married Women's Club. She promised me a nice audience and a friendly week-end. She named the date and as I saw that I had no engagement that week-end, I accepted and said that there would be no fee, no charge. I would do it for good-will and for the day in the country. But that it need not be all married women, it could be anyone and everyone and as far as I was concerned the more the merrier, and I would make them all laugh with a talk about this, that and the other, which would be ad lib and unrehearsed.

Today I received from the woman a short curt letter to the effect that she had discussed the matter with the vicar (how the heck he came into the married women's club, Gord knows) and he thinks I should be quite unsuitable and so the date is off and she doesn't wish to see *me*, but if Lizzie cares to go down for a day in August, they'd be glad to see her. Lizzie says, if Freddie is unsuitable, then Lizzie is as well, and that we are both particular whom we meet in Surrey or elsewhere! So I've written back to decline without thanks the invite for my landlady and to protest at the vicar saying I am unsuitable when he's never heard me speak and that no one has ever heard me say on a platform anything downright rude or in any way indecent, in my twelve years of public speaking.

¶ *April 1953*

Enterprise!

I am spending a pleasant week-end with my friend Margaret Walton and her family at Sidcup. It is Sunday morning and the time is just after eleven when I take a stroll down Halfway St. I am about half way down Halfway Street when I see an estate agents office named R. Duff & Partners. I stop to look at the pictures in the window of houses for sale and inspect the prices and details of some of them. It is not that I particully want to buy a house – I can easily find a house after I've got the wife – but there are worse and less interesting ways of spending a few moments than seeing the prices of houses. Most of them seem around the £2,500/£3,000 mark; but they look pretty good houses.

I am comparing one with the other when a man also gazing at the notices in the same window says: 'They seem rather expensive'. I say that it depends of course on the house but that £3,000 does seem a lot of money. He says: 'I've a nice house for sale. Mine is only £2,200. And you will notice the rates on these houses are around £23. Mine is only £19 and that's a big saving'. I can't myself see what a big saving £4 is when you are talking in thousands; but he's bigger than I am and besides, it's a pleasant sunny Sunday morning. He says: 'You can buy many cigarettes with £4. Yes, my house is very good value at £2,200. It's at 12 H— and you could come and see it right away!' I says that I don't carry that money with me Sunday mornings and wasn't in the right mood and then with a civil 'Good morning' I pass on.

I go into the town of Sidcup and I look in almost every shop window. I push leaflets about Fred Bason's Diary into the letter boxes of the local public library, Boots and all stationers. I am at least three quarters of an hour in Sidcup and then I make my way back to 75 Halfway St. for Luncheon. As I pass the estate agents I pause again, because I'd only seen one of the two windows when I'd been interupted by the house seller. There's a nice looking house at £2,500 that looks like a real love nest. A voice interupts my thoughts, 'Prices seem a little high, sir?' I nod. 'You interested in a house, sir?' I don't look round. I nod. Voice says, 'I've a nice house for sale freehold at 12 H—. Only £2,250.' I turn round and say 'And its only £19 rates and I could get a lot of cigarettes for £4! And you've got a bloody cheek to use the front of another man's shop in order to try to sell your house. And it's gone up £50. But I *do* admire your enterprise. Good morning!' And off I went, leaving him speechless.

¶ *A Date with Noel Coward*

It was a Red Letter occasion. The *first* time in my forty years of living (and I do live) I had on an evening dress and attended an English night club. I will tell you how it all came about.

I had heard that Noel Coward was appearing at The

Café de Paris in London's West End. He is 53, it was very likely to be his last cabaret appearance. So I wrote him a friendly letter, more or less in this strain.

'I gave you *Fred Bason's First Diary* and you wrote and said that you greatly enjoyed it. Then I gave you my second diary and I hope as how you enjoyed that Basonfull as well! I cannot be a stranger to you: indeed, I am not, for on over 65 occasions I have got your autograph, for yours happens to be one of the most swopable autographs in the far flung corners of the Empire. I have seen you in all your plays and attended the first nights of the plays you've written and not yourself appeared in. I've seen you in films and all manner of all-star shows. But I ain't *never* seen you in cabaret 'cause I have never been to a London Night club. Please would you allow me to be your guest at the Café de Paris? I wouldn't eat or drink, so as not to impose. I just want to hear you do your night-club act, so that I can say, in the days to come, that I had done just this.' I added that I wasn't cadging and was quite willing to give him or anyone else who pulled the strings *ten bob* for their trouble. I said finally that it was up to him. He could say 'No bloody fear' or 'Most certainly'. Wouldn't make the slightest difference to my admiration for his writings.

Three days later I got a nice kind letter from Charles Russell, his press representative on the behalf of Noel, thanking me for my *charming* letter and saying that Mr Coward would like me to come to the Café de Paris one night this week as his Cabaret season ends Sat. June 20. He suggests Thursdays night and 11.45 so as to have a drink with him before he appears at midnight. I replied (on a 1910 view of London postcard) that Thursday June 18th 1953 was a Date and I'd be there, tidy as possible.

Having posted that card, I got me to worrying a bit... *what about me attire?* I was to be Noel Coward's guest. I simply could not let down myself, Noel or Literature. I could not go in me rough old suit (16 years old) and a cap and say 'Wot cher, cock'. Being an extinguished author has its drawbacks. I hadn't thought of clothes in my keenness to hear Noel in his right surroundings. But now that I was agoing, it was quite a different matter. I was sure that evening dress was essential at the Café de Paris. Now, I am a small size in Cockneys and a stock size in small mens outfits. They didn't seem to have any evening togs down in the shops of Walworth Road. I didn't really expect them to. So I went up to Piccadilly and I saw a shop with smart second hand and misfit clothes, where they seemed to deal solely in evening kit. *But*, my golly, the prices! twelve quid and over! I just couldn't run to it. So I returned from Piccadilly and went around to a secondhand place in Bermondsey (of all places) where the boss was a fan of mine. Could he fit me up? Twenty minutes of suspense, and then a perfect fitting dinner jacket, almost made to measure. Price 12s 6d. But that was all he had. Pals of mine are real pals (for they know how I'd do the same for them) and he did some ringing up, and I went a couple of miles, and for 2s 6d I got a perfect fitting waistcoat which matched the jacket. Half the job done. But no one had any black evening-dress trouses – 'very scarce' they said. Scarce or not, I was *not* going to the Café de Paris without me blooming trouses on! I got on the phone to Peter Dale, another fan of mine. Desperate s.o.s. He has outfiting shops all over London. He's the director, can pull any strings. But with the greatest regret he had not a single pair of black trouses. He said he'd have gladly given them to me for such an occasion. Advised me to hire some. Gave me two addresses and told me to mention his name. But I was afraid. If I spoilt them hired trouses there would be the devil to pay. If I got me own and they were fully paid for I could do what I liked in them or with them. I was in a fix. Walking down the Old Kent Road, I came upon George Carter's shop. Very reliable old established firm. Last hope. Went me in and told them *all* about it. They did some hunting and lo and behold, up comes a perfect pair of black trouses the *match* of the jacket and the waistcoat. But they were much too long. What to do? Man very kind: cuts off the bit too much and with tailor's chalk marks exactly the turn up, where to tack, then press and all will be well, 'and your Landlady Liz can do that' . . . and Liz *did*.

Thursday I attended the Café de Paris; in 45/- trouses, 12s 6d jacket, 2s 6d waistcoat, plus a spotless white shirt (secondhand) and a natty black bow (16 years old) and Noel Coward said that I looked very smart indeed, and his pianist Norman Hackforth (same bloke in the basement of 'Twenty Questions') said I looked as if I had been poured into it, for it was all *a perfect fit*.

I arrived five minutes before 11.45 and was expected and was asked to wait. I gave up my hat and coat and noticed that I was *not* given a number or a receipt for either! Then a man called out, 'Boy' . . . and another called out 'Page' and a man in uniform came forward, who won't never see forty again and as a 'page' or a 'boy' was unquestionably more than slightly old. Even the man who asked for him asked if he really was the '*page*'. And he was! I sat me down on a comfortable chair and in two minutes Noel Coward and Charles Russell arrived. Noel flashed by. Charles shoke my hand warmly and asked me to wait a few moments, and then hurried after Noel.

I waited and as I waited, there came towards me a very stately lady. It was Lady Docker. First time I'd seen her in the flesh. She went into the ladies room which was right by the chair on which I was a sitting. I wanted to speak to her – to congratulate her on looking so beautifull – but she was gone into the room, and hadn't come out when Charles came for me and said Noel wanted to have a chat with me. We went almost round the balcony and there he was drinking a glass of *water*. He said he was delighted to meet me and what would I drink? I asked for a small whiskey – please and in a moment was given an exceedingly large glass of very good quality whiskey. Noel said: 'You are indeed a magnificent diariest, nothing escapes your eye, and your wit is superb. I read both your diaries and thoroughly enjoyed both of them'. I immediately asked if I could use the unsolicited testimonial and quote him, and he said that I could. He said that I'd been very wise and very brave to start a diary at 15 and keep it up, and I said that I'd acted on very good advice from two masters, Willie Maugham and James Agate. He said 'unequestionably Maugham is the master. You were wise to follow his advice . . . what was it?' And I told him that Maugham had said, so many many years ago, that I was to talk it all out aloud and if it sounded alright then it was alright and I was then to put it down and *never alter a word* of it.

I've always done just that. I extracted a promise from Noel that if I reached a fifth diary he would write the introduction to it, if we were still both alive. He said that he was now pruning his own latest book and that it would be ready next spring. He was not quite satisfied with it yet. I told him to make *sure* that it was bound in the same blue cloth as *Present Indicative* and was uniform in all other ways. He said he was of the same mind and would see to it, for he was all for books being uniform.

Noel then said, 'To think that I was once a professional dancer here! Ah me!' I asked if that was around the time Merle Oberon was a hostess here, and he said 'Oh no, long before even *that*'. I asked if he regretted his life and Noel said that he didn't and did I? 'Not for a moment', I answered. 'I'd do it all again and travel the same road. To regret is a waste of time'. 'You get no where ever so fast by regretting' were the words I used, and he repeated those words, and laughed, as if they were fresh ones to him.

Seeing as how he was merry and I'd got his interest, I told him a joke that I thought would make him go into his act in a few moments time in cheerful mood; and he really had *a very good laugh* over my little tale. This is it. There was a young woman who had so many children that she didn't know what to do, and another coming; so she went to the doctor and said, 'Doctor, I keep on having children, I don't know what on earth to do'. He studied her a moment and then said, 'You must take three asperins'. and she said, 'When, before or after?' And he said, 'Instead'.

Noel went to do his cabaret act, which lasted near an hour. He was in wonderful form. My golly, how he can put over a song! He first sang a medley of his own songs, like 'I'll see you again', 'Ladies of the Town'. After four songs I knew, he sung a very saucy one called 'Poor Uncle Harry' about a missionary who went wrong (shades of Maugham's Sadie Thompson), followed 'Harry' with a rustic one called 'Alice', also saucy. Then a song 'I wonder what became of . . .' which Noel said he not only wrote in India in 1944 but was brave enough to sing in India in 1944! I remember one line about Noel wondering what had happened to 'Frobisher of the 45th, who took to pig sticking in quite the wrong way. . . . I wonder what happened to him?' Then he sang, 'The Bonny Banks of Loch Lomond' with very many effects and a swing. Followed this with 'Half Caste Woman' which he wrote in 1929. (I liked this, for I was present the first night it was sung and danced.)

Then came his party piece 'Lets Fall in Love'. Wonderfull the people he suggested should fall in love. Grand Noel Coward song that. He then drank a glass of water and started off again with songs he would like to have written, such as 'Life is nothing without music'. . . 'Sweet and Low-down'. . . 'They all laughed when Christopher Columbus' . . . And then he returned to one of his own which he said that he wrote from the bottom of his heart, '*Don't* put your daughter on the stage, Mrs Worthington'. His act finished with *The Party's Over*. He bowed and run up the stairs from the floor to the balcony and to his room. He returned twice and bowed nicely. Norman Hackforth got up from the piano as Noel returned the second time.

Mrs Pat Hackforth was seated by my side during the

whole show (they'd been thoughtfull enough not to leave me alone) and I asked her if he ever did encores and she said she'd never known him to. When he'd sung *The Party's Over* the Party was really over. And I said that was wise. I didn't care for encores when a man had worked so hard to please. At the next table to me was Elizabeth Welch, the coloured singer, and she and I laughed the heartiest of the folks upstairs. Oh yes, I had lots of laughs.

I was chatting to Pat about the folks trying to dance on the small floor below when Charles Russell reappeared and asked if I'd enjoyed it. I *had* and so I said that I had.

If I had not, I'd have said not. It was *just* as I'd hoped and better if that don't sound too Irish. Charles asked me to have another drink, but I thought not as I was sure that I'd have to walk home and one extra large whiskey was quite enough for my little belly. I didn't want to be picked up by a woman or the police on such a wonderfull night.

Noel returned to us, had another glass of water, and went over to have a word with Elizabeth Welch. I had a chat with Norman Hackforth. I said that it must be hard and difficult work to be Noel's pianist, and he agreed that it was *work*. He then said that I looked nice in my evening dress, and I said it was a novelty for me but usual for him to have evening kit. His wife said that he was seldom out of it; indeed it was his boiler suit. Witty lady and so pretty. Noel returned to his table and I congratulated him very, very sincerely on a great show by a great showman.

Having drunk his fourth glass of water, Noel said that, what with the Shaw play at the Haymarket and this show, he was working very hard – too hard – and had to get off to bed. He said I was not to hurry myself, and if I wanted

another drink I was to order it in his name. I shook hands
with him and with the other kind folk who had made my
night so enjoyable. I was now left alone. It was about 1.30.
I asked a strange lady who was just pasing when the place
shut down, and she said 'Twoish'. She then said she knew
me; but she pronounced my name Bazon. She was pretty
and youngish, 23 or so. She sat down and I looked over
the balcony and asked her what it cost to be down there,
as I was an entire stranger. She said that it was £2 for
supper upstairs and that did not include tips or wines. 'Call
it £5 for two in this balcony. It's more downstairs for
everything.'

I left the Café de Paris at ten to two and tried to get
a taxi. But none would brave the perils of Walworth, so
I walked home. The air was cool and pleasant and I did not
hurry. Reached home at 152 Westmoreland Road SE 17
at exactly ten to three. It had taken me *one* exact hour
to walk from the *sublime* of Café de Paris to the *Blimey*
of Walworth. I shut the front door with great care and
as I did so Lizzie switched on the light in her bedroom
and said, 'Are you sober?' I said that I was most certainly
very sober, but that I'd had a lovely time. She said, 'Well,
leave it to the morning to tell me all about it', and I said,
that it *was* the morning, very much so! Well, five to three
is morning. It's the latest I've been out in years except for
the Arts Ball. I just couldn't sleep. I drank the hot milk
which Liz had so thoughtfully placed in a thermos flask at
my bedside. I was still excited, sleep wouldn't come to me,
so I sat me up in bed and I wrote all this that you've read:
took me another hour, and then I was tired and sleeped a
very good sound and honest sleep.

¶ *July 1953*

Dear kind Hilaire Belloc has died as the result of an accident. I only met him four or five times in his long career. I got his autograph when we were both guests at Balliol College. I was in a wheelchair – injured in raids. We had 15 minutes chat and he said of his own books he liked *Cautionary Tales* and *Path to Rome*. I said *Pongo and the Bull* was perhaps my favourite. I recalled that, when Shaw and Chesterton were debating at the Kingsway Hall and H.B. was in the chair, Shaw said 'Chesterton has completely missed the point' and, like lightening, Belloc came back with: 'But the art of a duel *is* to miss the point'. Oh yes, H.B. was a witty man. His power was in his huge range of talent. Belloc was a great man who carried fame very gracefully. Will be long remembered with respect.

¶ *July 18th 1953*

I cannot remember it ever raining so hard in my part of London as it did between six and seven this afternoon. It simply poured down and gave me a pain in the belly. (Storms always upset me. It's the electricity in the air.) Last time, I was in such heavy rain was in Yugoslavia a couple of years ago, but today's beat even that. Some houses at the Elephant were struck – fortunately not so very seriously. I'd been out till five on a book-hunting tour. Mainly to seek *Curiousities of Literature* by Disraeli for a U.S.A. client. Most times you can pick up this book with ease. Today not a single copy around, although I went for miles. However, it was not a wasted journey, for I pur-

chased *Travellers* by Strong, two books by Ann Bridge,
Creatures of Circumstance by Maugham, a book by Farnol
and one by S. P. B. Mais called *The Writing of English*. I
will read the Mais one and if I sell the others, the profit
from it will allow me to keep the English one free. During
the great storm I sat at my typewriter making out a list of
'Books for sale' which incorporated the above. I then typed
envelopes and dispatched the lists to Bethnal Green Public
Library and to Kensington Public Library. Yes, diary, a
copy of the same list. I know from experience that what
sells in Kensington don't sell in Bethnal Green and so their
needs and their orders never clash and it saves a lot of
time. It's still a great storm and I felt like nothing on earth.
Haven't the courage to put radio on in case we get struck
by lightening. So to kill time I am now going to write to
Walt Disney at the Dorchester and invite him here to tea.
There is one other man I'd like to entertain here – J. B.
Priestley, always so nice to me.

¶ *September 18th 1953*

This evening I went to the R. L. Stevenson Club, a very
small and select collection of folks who enjoy the writings
of Stevenson and who meet occasionally to discuss them
and have a pleasant evening. I was only the guest for this
one night. I have no great love for Stevenson, and no time
to go often to clubs; and I refuse to join any club where I
cannot play a real part and attend reasonably regularly.

But I had real pleasure out of going to this club, because
I met a dear old man aged 86 named Clive Holland. We had
a nice conversation, and I learnt that he knew Thomas

Hardy and Miss Braddon quite well, and that, when he was around sixteen, he had many conversations with Robert Louis Stevenson. Probably he is the only man still living who has spoken to Stevenson and certainly he is a much treasured member of this club.

As I'd read several books on Hardy, I didn't want a personal recollection of him; so I asked Mr Holland if he could tell me something about Miss Braddon that was nice to recall. After a moment's thought, he said that she was very fond of giving literary parties to the up and coming musicians, artists, and literary men of her day. Not for the famous, but for the promising ones, and the choice was her own. In consequence, people who were asked to her 'dos' felt a little proud of themselves. At least Miss Braddon thought that they were promising. But she had a nice colourful rule that when she left after dinner with the other females, so that the men could be alone over their cigars and wine, it was always the custom for the men to line up on either side of the door, just as a sort of guard of honour; and Miss Braddon with her stick would slowly move down between the rows of men looking neither to left nor to right. When she got to the door she would turn round and with a neat simple bow, would put on a brilliant smile for all the men, and then tap her stick once and the door would open and out she would go . . . followed by the rest of the ladies. He said that he would never forget Miss Braddon's slow, graceful walk. The dignity of it had to be seen; it could never be disturbed. Mr Holland said that he met R.L.S. many times at Bournemouth and they went for walks to Stevenson's favourite spot in England, just by Alum Chine. Sixty years ago this spot was covered with heather and when Holland asked R.L.S. why it was his favourite spot, Stevenson said that, as he looked towards the Purbeck Hills, it reminded him of Scotland and yet was good for his health outside Scotland. He said that the route for a walk was always to the same place, some two hundred yards from Alum Chine and that Stevenson never seemed to tire of it. I asked if R.L.S. wore his hair long even in those days, and Mr Holland said, 'Yes, just like Buffalo Bill did'. He also said that Stevenson had a pleasant voice. So had Mr Holland and I was truly delighted to meet him. He was also pleased to know me, because I was able to prove that I knew the writings of Clive Holland...but outside *Treasure Island* I am very doubtful if I could have proved that I knew the writings of Stevenson.

¶ *December 1953*

It gives me sadness to record the deaths during the year of six of my boy-hood film star favourites. Men I really admired and saved up my pennies to see many times. But for some reason or another I did not ever get (or thought to get) their autographs and now it is too late. William Farnum, who was so good in early Zane Grey Westerns like *Riders of the Purple Sage*. A real he-man and late in his life played innumerable character parts. He must have been a film star all of 40 years. And he didn't ever leave a book of memories! Francis Ford, who was in many early serials like *The Exploits of Elaine* and *The Broken Coin*. I remember his flat nose and his big fists. Sort of E. Flynn when I was 12 years old. Herbert Rawlinson, who was so good looking, tall and had wavy hair and played everything from he-man fighting to delicate love scenes. Roland Young was a rather funny man on the films but a very touchy and unagreeable man off stage. I met him once – once was enough. He was downright rude – still, I laughed at him and remember his very original style. Lewis Stone, a darling man – charming, gentlemanly, intelligent, stylish. A real film star. Of these six Lewis Stone is the one I shall miss the most. The last film I saw him in was *All the Brothers were Valiant* with Robert Taylor and Stewart Granger. A well made film from a story by Ben Ames Williams. I expect that Robert Taylor will be on the films for all of forty years unless something untold happens. I *do* hope that he will write a book of his recollections before the end. What a great book of invaluable memories and recollections of the early days of filmland William Farnum could have written – and now too late. I hope my new favourite film star Robert Taylor *will* write a book.

On Christmas Day of all days Lee Shubert died. He was a huge power in U.S.A. Theatreland. He could make or break anyone. Indeed my pals say he had too much power. Well, where ever is he now? He has *no* power and is a beginner in the last row of the chorus. And he *now* knows that there are no pockets in shrouds.

¶ *Thursday, March 25, 1954*

Answering an S.O.S. telegram, I spoke to the Round-tablers of Petersfield this night. I would not have accepted the engagement at any other town in England because Thursday is my 'At Home Day' when my fans call to, as it were, sit at the foot of the master! But Petersfield holds

Bitter Sweet memoirs and it was just thirteen years ago
that I was last there. Before I did my talk I asked a kindness
and I was driven in a posh car just outside Petersfield. I
went to enquire if K. was still alive. I loved K. for years.
Loved...that's mild. I adored her and would gladly have
lived or died with her – till she got religious mania. Yes,
K. is still alive and still single. By her side I could have
found inspiration for great writing. I am glad I did *not* see
my old love. A man does not forget a true love. I would
not marry her now at any price, but I shall never forget
her. I wish her well! It was a sentimental journey at a time
when I was mentally ill and so tired.

¶ *January 1954*

Be Carefull What You Say!

I think it might be an eye-opener to my fans to know
what happens after a very ordinary B.B.C. radio date.

January 1st, 1954. I spoke in 'Woman's Hour' and said
that my New Year Resolution would be to read *one* page
of the Bible each day of this year – because I'd never read
the Bible. That *was* my intention. I got 306 letters all from
entire strangers giving me in extremely long letters much
advice upon what to read from the Bible and what *not*
to read. *Plus* 197 pamphlets, guides, text books and aids to
reading the Bible, from weird and wonderfull societies and
groups of Christians. *Plus* a proposal of marriage from a
lady who said she could guide my life and my reading
and save my soul all at the same time! *Plus* a lady at Clacton
offering to become my secretary, *plus* a request to speak
at five Mothers' Meetings in and around London (no fee

mentioned) plus a request to speak to the Young Conservatives of Beckenham.

And *final* plus, a really astounding letter. I sent it back to the young lady. By golly, I do now wish I'd kepted it! This lady said she was 43 and looked no more than 34 and was a Christian. She said she worked at Windsor but was on holiday at her home in Tottenham. Would I meet her next Thursday at the 96 bus stop? She'd be wearing a green baize coat and no hat. She would then take me somewhere nice and *pray for my salvation*.

She didn't explain where the 96 bus stop was. She didn't state a time. I replied that I thought me salvation was getting along pretty fair and I didn't feel inclined to go to an unknown bus stop on a bitter cold day – even to go somewhere nice. But that I hoped her salvation looked as young as she did and was doing as nicely as mine!

Nett result of all that I've told you was that after ten days I got so utterly confused that I returned the Bible I'd had on loan (No, I didn't own a Bible) and started reading *Dr Thorndyke's Famous Cases* by my one time friend R. Austin Freeman. Reckon Dr Thorndyke would have made quite a case out of the girl at Tottenham. Next time I give a new year resolution it will be to collect a diamond ring once a month! I wonder *what* will happen?

¶ *January 1955*

I've reluctantly decided never again to read an un-solicited manuscript. I shall return any unread. They only want their own good opinion endorsed. When you tell 'em your honest opinion they are extremely rude!

¶ *Finale 1955*
  Southwark Serenade

Its evening. I am seated at the window of my study trying to read. Across the road is the local school, and above the school is a bonfire of sunset to bring to a close a lovely summer's evening. This sunset casts a glow on the dear little children, who in their dozens are screaming, both in the playground of the school and in the street outside my window. Children everywhere. It is said that no man is a real man around this part of London until he's given his wife four or five children ... and there are a lot of real men in the neighbourhood.

Just below me there is a sweet little boy with a spade that's taller than him. Alas for him and for others, there is today no sand or mud so he is just amusing his sweet self by bashing the spade down on the pavement and making a noise. This noise, no doubt, amuses him; but it would wake the dead, only this isn't a day for dying. Nearby a boy is throwing large bricks up into the air and letting them fall to pieces on the ground. I am willing to lay six to four that he don't know what game he is playing — except that it also makes a noise and a dust.

One dear little boy has kicked violently at the door of his home at least six times in the last hour, and screamed out for his mother to come down so that he can go in and get a cup of water; and she comes down everytime and lets him in. That's mother love. Now he wants to go in to *make* water, so down she's coming again. She's a little tired, but down she comes, I can hear her above the din of a nearby radio set. The people who own this radio are very kind people and love to share their pleasures and so I have no need whatever to put my own radio on. I can always hear theirs with the greatest comfort – or discomfort as the case may be. The screams and the radio make quite a din. All part of the pattern of the serenade.

Ten doors away there is a Public House. Later this night, when that pub shuts, the clients will bid each other Good Night. They will not just say one Goodnight for *all*, there will be Good Night for Bill, Joe and Jim, and Good Night for Maud and Mary. As they draw away from each other, the Goodnights will be louder and louder, just in case Mary did not hear Jim say 'Good Night Mary' and Mary may take umbrage and be offended the next night, because Jim said Good Night to Maud and Maud's mother in law but left her out. No one knows *why* she should be offended but thats the Way of Southwark, quick to take offence. The loudest Goodnights start up just below my window and if I was asleep they would wake me up so I don't attempt to sleep till the Goodnight session is over. Sometimes they have a last minute talk just outside my window and you *do* hear a lot of juicy gossip on these occasions and the things that Sarah does is Everybodies business – and what a business.

Nearby there are dog lovers. These dogs can howl from six in the morning to six the next morning and no one is expected to mind. Why they bark so frequently is a mystery, unless it's the cats. There are a lot of cats in Southwark. The said cats seemed to be sex-starved or something. They never seem to be at all particular over which cat they take into the coal sheds. Perhaps it is the sex parties of the cats which disturb the dogs, and who can blame them?

Then I must not forget the chickens, although they are mostly cocks and they seem to want their breakfast at four in the morning and make no bones about asking for it with lusty crows. It's about eight before they cease or the start of the days radio drowns their calls. Once they have woken you there is no more sleep. It's impossible.

There are of course the pigeons. They ought to get a write up. Two or three wouldn't matter, but the sound of forty or so can be a little disturbing to everyone else but the owners of them. They make a weird noise and that noise disturbs the cats and dogs and they answer back. So there are many bird arguments and no one gets anywhere.

Every evening somewhere closeby, a would-be pianist is learning to play *Butterflies in the Rain*. It's a very pretty tune, but not the way she plays it, and she's been playing it wrong every night now for around six months. Yes, every night. Sometimes I wish that she was at the Albert Hall or some where else. If she goes on at the rate she is now going on I reckon she will play this piece in seven years time. Will I be alive to hear it?

At the top of this road there is a railway line, and when there is a little quiet you can hear the trains. I have not heard a train for the past five weeks. The Old Kent Road is at one end of the same road and the Walworth Road is at the other. They are very busy roads, with a constant roar of traffic; but you never hear the traffic above the roar of the dear little children at play.

Of course, I must not fail to mention dear old Father Thames who keeps on rolling along, with all manner of boats and barges on his back, hooting by night and by day.

Glad to state that the boy with the spade has put the spade down. Now he has a large muffin bell instead. And the sweet little boy next door has had so much cold water that he now has a medium belly ache and screaming blue murder! The bugles have just started up. Oh, I forget all about the bugles. Just at the back of us is a church hall used by Boy Scouts and others, and the dear boys practice on bugles. I never know what the heck they are trying to play; but, by golly, they do *try* to play it, and on hefty lungs at that.

The boys of the village have just started a fight with the boys from the next street. It will go on for some hours. It starts rather like this (in case you are still with me).

'I dare yer.'

'You what?'

'I dare yer.'

'You dare *me?*'

'I dare yer to 'it me!'

'You dare me . . . *me!*'

'Why, I'll mark you wif a razor, that's what I'll do.'

'You and who else?'

'Me – only *me!*'

'I dare yer.'

Repeat . . . Repeat! It will be a lovely fight when it gets started unless the police come along in time. The residents dont stand an earthly because if you tries to break it up both sides start on you. And I do like me window glass intact. But still, the boys have got to have their fun, havn't they?

I notice now that the girls of the town are passing and the wolf cries are out. But the girls can give as good as they get, often better. And nine venders of toffee apples and ice cream have screamed out their wares as they have passed by in the last 37 minutes. You wouldn't think that that there was enough trade for nine of them – but they will be back again and again.

At two tomorrow morning the milk lorry will pass by my window with its rattle of milk in wire crates, and will be delivered to the milk shop along the road. If you are just dropping off to sleep, its guaranteed to wake you up, and if you are in your first sleep and haven't put the ear plugs in you will be woken up. It's all part of the service. Some folks *have* to be up at two in the morning...some do!

At midnight the car that stands for hours two doors away will start up after the owner of it has slammed the doors shut. I will take six to four that the door slamming will wake you up as well. Still, you *do* get two hours between the car and the milk lorry so what are you grumbling about?

Me – I am not grousing. Its been part of the music for years and years. The children have now left the play-ground across the street and the caretaker is locking up. The children will play outside this house for at least another hour – or like daddy and mummy, they will take an hour to part from their bosom pals with 'Goodnights' and strict instructions not to be late in the morning. Some old folks have just passed by. They are going to the work house just past the milkshop. The boys of the village pass rude remarks about them and the old folks say nothing –

if they are wise. They let the fighting teams get worked up past the 'Dare you' stage. A very pretty girl has passed by. You will find her in an hours time just off Bond Street and you can have a short time with her for 30s! But if you suggested the same thing to her as she passed your window she'd slap your face! She has her pitch *and* her pride.

The fight has now commenced. They have pieces of wood and stones, and I would even say much worse things in their pockets. There won't be any silence for awhile now, so I will leave this and go and get a *double* sleep pill – that with ear plugs, plus the blanket over my head, may get me a little sleep. But after all this is a quiet and respectable neighbourhood compared to some. It's been my home town for better or worse for forty years and I wouldn't change it or move from it for anything – anything except a really nice lady. When I find the woman I leave Walworth for ever.